chic knits for stylish babies

chic knits for stylish babies

65 charming patterns for the first year

Patricia Wagner, editor-in-chief of Modes & Travaux
photography by Jean-François Chavanne

Watson-Guptill Publications / New York

our thanks

To all the designers whose talent has brought these patterns to life: Patricia Antoine, Aline Faillet, Juliette Liétar, and Dany Ribailler. To Véronique Linard, who, stitch by stitch, wrote out the instructions, and to Olivier Ribailler, who drew the diagrams.

Thanks, too, to the yarn manufacturers—Phildar, Bouton d'Or, and Anny Blatt—without whom these creations would not be possible.

Marabout warmly thanks Stella Ruiz and Patricia Adrian for their invaluable collaboration.

Interior design: Nathalie Delhaye

Copyright © 2007 by Marabout, Paris

First published in the United States
by Watson-Guptill Publications,
a division of VNU Business Media, Inc.,
770 Broadway, New York, N.Y. 10003
www.watsonguptill.com

ISBN-10: 0-8230-9995-4
ISBN-13: 978-0-8230-9995-5

Library of Congress Control Number: 2006939195

Manufactured in China

First printing, 2007

1 2 3 4 5 / 11 10 09 08 07

skill level

The number of stars that follow the title of each pattern indicate its level of difficulty:

★ Beginner/Easy. Uses basic knit and purl stitches; may require repetitive stitch patterns and simple color changes. Shaping and finishing are minimal/simple.

★ ★ Intermediate. Uses a variety of stitches, such as basic cables and simple intarsia, with mid-level shaping and finishing.

★ ★ ★ Experienced. Involves intricate stitch patterns, techniques, and dimension, such as non-repeating patterns, multicolored techniques, detailed shaping, and refined finishing.

foreword

With your baby about to arrive any day now, you can gently prepare for this unique time by lovingly knitting beautiful garments in soft pastel colors for your special baby. Just close your eyes . . .

Can you picture him or her lying there, gurgling and wriggling in a crib? Now the colors become clearer, stronger. Keep your eyes closed for just a little longer and picture a few months later. Crawling around, he or she is discovering the world, the grass, the ground, the colors of nature. Then, at last, standing up proudly, wearing high-fashion clothes in bright, striking colors. A spirited baby, an adventurous baby, a smart (stylish) baby . . . what do you dream of for your newborn? Now, open your eyes and count the stitches while you wait for the great day to arrive.

Patricia Wagner
editor-in-chief of Modes & Travaux

contents

all-weather babies

Irish leprechaun

Irish leprechaun

A cable-knit outfit straight from the homeland of leprechauns and sprites.

Sweater ★★

Sizes
(3 months) 6 months [12 months]

Materials
Any acrylic-and-lamb's wool-blend fingering weight yarn, such as Phildar's *Super Baby* (70% acrylic/30% lamb's wool; $^{7}/_{8}$oz/25g = 117yd/107m) in olive green (*Olive/110*)
3 months: 6 balls (702yd/642m)
6 months: 6 balls (702yd/642m)
12 months: 8 balls (936yd/856m)
1 pair each #4/3.5mm and #6/4mm knitting needles, or sizes needed to obtain gauge
1 double-pointed cable needle
6 small wooden 4-hole buttons

Stitches
Double Rib: *K2, P2*, rep from * to *.
Moss Stitch: *Row 1:* *K1, P1*, rep from * to *. *Row 2:* work the sts as in the previous row. *Row 3:* *P1, K1*, rep from * to *. *Row 4:* As Row 2. Rep these 4 rows for patt.
Cable pattern (see chart): Cables cover 34 sts across the panel. K the small cable on each side over 6 rows and the center cable over 8 rows.
4 sts crossed to the right: Sl 2 sts onto the cn and place it behind the work, K the next 2 sts, then the 2 sts on the cn.
4 sts crossed to the left: Sl 2 sts onto the cn and place it in front of the work, K the next 2 sts, then the 2 sts on the cn.

Gauges
22 stitches and 33 rows to a 4"/10cm square knit in Moss St on #6/4mm needles with the yarn doubled.
Cables: 5½"/14cm
  Take the time to make a gauge swatch, which is especially important if you are substituting the suggested yarn.
If necessary, change needle sizes to obtain the correct gauge.

Making the sweater
The yarn should be knit double throughout.

• Back
Using #4/3.5mm needles, CO (54) 58 [62] sts and work ¾"/2cm in Double Rib. Change to #6/4mm needles and cont as foll:
(10) 12 [14] sts in Moss St, 34 sts in Cable patt, and (10) 12 [14] sts in Moss St.
  When piece measures (6"/15cm) 6¾"/17cm [7½"/19cm], beg shaping armholes: BO 3 sts at beg of next 2 rows, then 1 st at beg of next 4 rows.**
  When piece measures (9½"/24cm) 10¾"/27cm [11¾"/30cm], beg shaping neck: BO (22) 24 [26] sts in the center of next row and complete each side separately.
  When piece measures (9¾"/25cm) 11"/28cm [12¼"/31cm], cont in Double Rib, beg with P1, on the rem (11) 12 [13] sts.
  When piece measures (10¾"/27cm) 11¾"/30cm [13"/33cm], BO in rib.

• Front
Work as for back to **.
  When piece measures (8¼"/21cm) 9½"/24cm [10¾"/27cm], beg shaping neck: BO the (8) 10 [12] sts in the center of next row and complete each side separately. On alt rows, beg at neck edge, BO 3 sts once, 2 sts twice, and 1 st twice.
  Work even until piece measures (9"/23cm) 10¼"/26cm [11½"/29cm], then cont in Double Rib on the rem (11) 12 [13] sts, making two 2-st buttonholes on the 3rd row, the 1st buttonhole

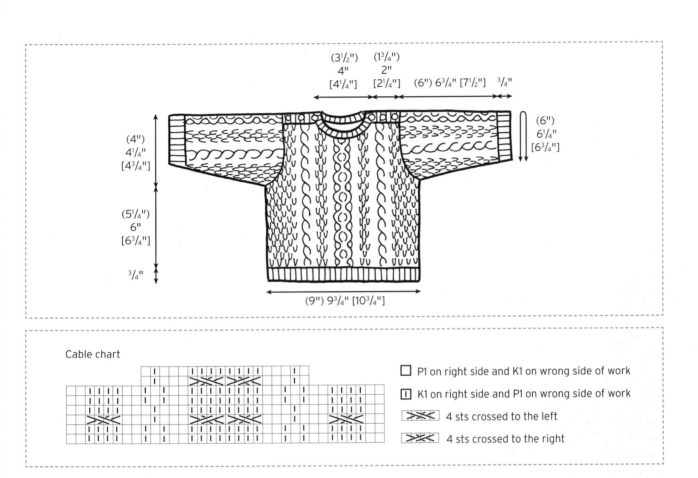

Cable chart

☐ P1 on right side and K1 on wrong side of work

⊡ K1 on right side and P1 on wrong side of work

▷▷◁ 4 sts crossed to the left

▷▷◁ 4 sts crossed to the right

2 sts from the edge and the 2nd after (3) 4 [4] sts. Cont even until work measures (9¾"/25cm) 11"/28cm [12¼"/31cm]. BO in rib for the shoulder.

• Sleeves

Using #4/3.5mm needles, CO (36) 38 [40] sts and work ¾"/2cm in Double Rib. Change to #6/4mm needles and cont as foll: (1) 2 [3] sts in Moss St, 34 sts in Cable patt, and (1) 2 [3] sts in Moss St, inc 1 st at each end of every 6th row (6) 7 [8] times.

When piece measures (6"/15cm) 6¾"/17cm [7½"/19cm], BO 3 sts once and 1 st twice at beg of each row, then BO the rem (38) 42 [46] sts.

Finishing

Using #4/3.5mm needles, pick up and K (24) 26 [30] sts evenly along the front neck and work ¾"/2cm in Double Rib, beg with (P1) K2 [K2], making a 2-st buttonhole 2 sts from the edge on the 2nd row. BO in rib.

Using #4/3.5mm needles, pick up and K (34) 36 [40] sts evenly along the back neck and work ¾"/2cm in Double Rib, beg with (K2) P1 [P1]. BO in rib.

Match up the edges of the shoulders and sew the shoulder sides. Fit and sew the sleeves and sides of the sweater. Sew the buttons onto the back shoulder bands.

Pants ★★

Sizes

(3 months) 6 months [12 months]

Materials

Any acrylic-and-lamb's wool-blend fingering weight yarn, such as Phildar's *Super Baby* (70% acrylic/30% lamb's wool; ⅞oz/25g = 117yd/107m) in colors: A (terra-cotta–*Renne/123*) and B (olive green–*Olive/110*)

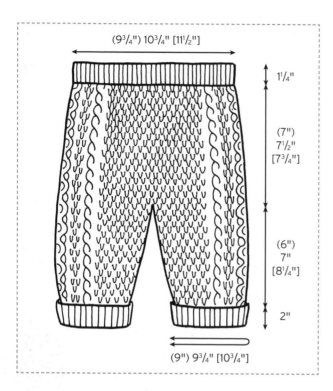

(9³/₄") 10³/₄" [11¹/₂"]

1¹/₄"

(7")
7¹/₂"
[7³/₄"]

(6")
7"
[8¹/₄"]

2"

(9") 9³/₄" [10³/₄"]

When piece measures (7³/₄"/20cm) 9"/23cm [10¹/₄"/26cm], make the crotch: BO 2 sts at beg of next 2 rows and 1 st at beg of next 6 rows, then cont even.

When piece measures (15"/38cm) 16¹/₂"/42cm [18¹/₄"/46cm], change to #4/3.5mm needles and work 1¹/₄"/3cm of Single Rib, then BO in rib.

Work 2nd leg to match the 1st leg.

• Finishing
Sew the back and front crotch seams.

Sew the leg seams, changing the stitching to right side out from halfway down the ribbing at the ankle to allow for the cuff.

Thread a few rows of elastic through the waistband ribbing.

Hat ★★

Sizes
(3 months) 6 months [12 months]

Materials
Any acrylic-and-lamb's wool-blend fingering weight yarn, such as Phildar's *Super Baby* (70% acrylic/30% lamb's wool;

3 months: 6 balls A and 2 balls B
6 months: 8 balls A and 2 balls B
12 months: 8 balls A and 2 balls B
1 pair each #4/3.5mm and #6/4mm knitting needles, or sizes needed to obtain gauge
1 double-pointed cable needle
Narrow elastic

Stitches
Single Rib: *K1, P1*, rep from * to *.
Double Rib: See sweater instructions.
Moss Stitch: See sweater instructions.
Cables: See sweater instructions.

Gauge
See sweater instructions.

Making the pants
The yarn should be knit double throughout.

• Legs
Using #4/3.5mm needles and B, CO (54) 58 [62] sts and work 2"/5cm Double Rib. Change to #6/4mm needles and A and cont as foll: (10) 12 [14] sts in Moss St, 34 sts in Cable patt and (10) 12 [14] sts in Moss St. Inc 1 st at each end of (every 6th row 7 times) every 8th row 7 times [every 8th row 4 times, then every foll 10th row 3 times].

⅞oz/25g = 117yd/107m) in colors: A (terra-cotta–*Renne/123*) and B (olive green–*Olive/110*)
For all sizes: 2 balls A and 2 balls B
1 pair each #4/3.5mm and #6/4mm knitting needles, or sizes needed to obtain gauge
1 double-pointed cable needle

Stitches
Double Rib: See sweater instructions.
Moss Stitch: See sweater instructions.
Cables: See sweater instructions.

Gauge
See sweater instructions.

Making the hat
The yarn should be knit double throughout.
Using #4/3.5mm needles and B, CO (38) 42 [46] sts and work 2"/5cm in Double Rib.
Change to #6/4mm needles and A and cont as foll: (2) 4 [6] sts in Moss St, 34 sts in Cable patt and (2) 4 [6] sts in Moss St.
When piece measures (7"/18cm) 7½"/19cm [7¾"/20cm], BO. Work 2nd piece to match the 1st piece.

Finishing
Sew the 2 pieces together, changing stitching to right side out from halfway down the ribbing to allow for the brim.
Make 2 tassels using 17 strands of B, each 6¼"/16cm in length, and sew a tassel to each top corner of the hat.

Scarf and mittens ★

Materials
Any acrylic-and-lamb's wool-blend fingering weight yarn, such as Phildar's *Super Baby* (70% acrylic/30% lamb's wool; ⅞oz/25g = 117yd/107m) in colors: A (terra-cotta–*Renne/123*) and B (olive green–*Olive/110*)
For the set: 2 balls A or B and a small amount of contrast color
1 pair each #4/3.5mm and #6/4mm knitting needles, or sizes needed to obtain gauge

Stitches
Double Rib: See sweater instructions.
Moss Stitch: See sweater instructions.

Gauge
See sweater instructions.

Making the scarf and mittens
The yarn should be knit double throughout.

• Scarf
Using #6/4mm needles and A or B, CO 18 sts and work (27"/68cm) 28½"/73cm [30½"/78cm] in Moss St, then BO.
Make 4 tassels using 17 strands of the contrast color, each 6¼"/16cm in length, and sew one to each corner of the scarf.

• Mittens
Using #4/3.5mm needles and B, CO (16) 18 [18] sts and work 1¼"/3cm of Double Rib. Change to #6/4mm needles and A or B and cont in Moss St for another 2"/5cm, then dec 1 st at each end of every alt row (4) 5 [5] times. BO the rem 8 sts.
Make a 2nd piece to match, then sew them together.
Make 2 tassels (see scarf pattern) in A or B and sew one onto each mitten.

English style

Truly elegant, in the misty colors of the British moors.

Hooded jacket ★★

Sizes
(3 months) 6 months [12 months]

Materials
Any acrylic-and-wool-blend worsted weight yarn, such as Phildar's *Quiétude* (50% acrylic/50% combed wool; 1¾oz/50g = 98yd/90m) in A (copper–*Kraft/101*)

Any pure wool light worsted weight yarn, such as Phildar's *Pure Laine* (100% wool; 1¾oz/50g = 115yd/108m) in B (green–*Romarin/304*)

Any acrylic-and-lamb's wool-blend fingering weight yarn, such as Phildar's *Super Baby* (70% acrylic/30% lamb's wool; ⅞oz/25g = 117yd/107m) in C (dusky pink–*Bruyère/112*)

Any wool-and-acrylic-blend sport weight yarn, such as Phildar's *Phil'Laine* (51% wool/49% acrylic; 1¾oz/50g = 138yd/126m) in D (gold–*Maïs/055*)

3 months: 3 balls A and a small amount of the other 3 colors
6 months: 4 balls A and a small amount of the other 3 colors
12 months: 4 balls A and a small amount of the other 3 colors
1 pair #6/4mm knitting needles, or size needed to obtain gauge
1 spare needle or stitch holder
4 small wooden 2-hole toggles

Stitches
Stockinette Stitch: K 1 row, P 1 row.
Moss Slip Stitch: *Row 1:* K1, *sl 1 purlwise, K1*, rep from * to *. *Row 2:* *K1, wyif, sl 1 purlwise*, rep from * to *, K1. *Row 3:* K1, *K1, sl 1 purlwise*, rep from * to *. *Row 4:* wyif, *sl 1 purlwise, K1*, rep from * to *, K1. Rep these 4 rows for patt.

Seed Stitch: *Row 1:* *K1, P1*, rep from * to *. *Row 2:* *P1, K1*, rep from * to *. Rep these 2 rows for patt.
Left-slanting decrease (SKP): Sl 1 knitwise, K1, PSSO.

Gauge
19 stitches and 27 rows to a 4"/10cm square knit in Stockinette St with yarn A on #6/4mm needles.

Take the time to make a gauge swatch, which is especially important if you are substituting the suggested yarn.
If necessary, change needle sizes to obtain the correct gauge.

Making the hooded jacket
The back and fronts are knit together.

Using #6/4mm needles and A, CO (89) 97 [105] sts and work 8 rows in Moss Slip St, alternating 2 rows B, 2 rows C, 2 rows D, and 2 rows A, then cont even in Stockinette St.

When piece measures (5½"/14cm) 6¼"/16cm [7"/18cm], beg shaping raglans. For the right front, work on the 1st (23) 25 [27] sts, putting the rem sts on a spare needle or stitch holder.
To shape the raglan, beg at armhole edge, BO 3 sts once, then dec 1 st every alt row (10 times) 11 times [11 times, then dec 1 st every 4th row once], using SKP to dec.

When piece measures (17½"/19cm) 8¾"/22cm [9¾"/25cm], beg shaping neck: On alt rows, beg at neck edge, dec (3 sts twice and 2 sts once) 4 sts once, 3 sts once, and 1 st twice [4 sts twice and 1 st twice], then BO the rem 2 sts after the final dec for the raglan.

For the left front, pick up and K (23) 25 [27] sts on the left and complete to match right front, reversing the shapings and dec by K2tog.

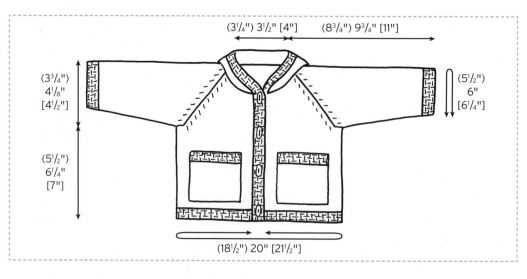

(3¼") 3½" [4"]   (8¾") 9¾" [11"]

(3¾") 4⅛" [4½"]

(5½") 6" [6¼"]

(5½") 6¼" [7"]

(18½") 20" [21½"]

For the back, pick up the (43) 47 [51] sts rem in the center, BO 3 sts at beg of next 2 rows, then dec 1 st at each end of every alt row (10) 11 [11] times and dec 1 st at each end every 4th row (once) once [twice] (use K2tog to dec on RH side and SKP to dec on LH side). After dec for the final time, BO the rem (15) 17 [19] sts.

• Right sleeve

Using #6/4mm needles and A, CO (27) 29 [31] sts and work 8 rows in Moss Slip St, alternating the rows of colors as for the front, then cont even in Stockinette St, inc 1 st at each end of every 4th row (4 times) 4 times [5 times] and 1 st every 6th row (twice) 3 times [3 times].

When piece measures (6"/15cm) 6¾"/17cm [7½"/19cm], beg shaping raglans. BO 3 sts at beg of next 2 rows, then shape RH side dec as for the front and LH side dec as for the back. After dec for the last time for the front, BO 6 sts every alt row twice on RH side.

• Left sleeve

Work as for right sleeve, reversing shapings.

• Hood

Using #6/4mm needles and A, CO (64) 68 [72] sts and work even in Stockinette St.

When piece measures (6¼"/16cm) 6¾"/17cm [7"/18cm], BO 10 sts at beg of next 4 rows, then BO the rem (24) 28 [32] sts.

• Pockets

Using #6/4mm needles and A, CO 16 and work 2½"/6cm in Stockinette St, then ½"/1.5cm in Seed St, and BO in patt.

Finishing

Fit in and sew the sleeves. Sew the hood and stitch it to the neck opening.

Using B, pick up and K (47) 54 [62] sts evenly along the right front, then (63) 67 [71] sts along the edge of the hood and (47) 54 [62] sts along the left front. Work 8 rows in Moss Slip St, alternating 2 rows D, 2 rows C, 2 rows B, and 2 rows A: *Row 1:* P1, *sl 1 purlwise, P1*, rep from * to *. *Row 2:* *P1, wyib sl 1 purlwise*, P1. *Row 3:* P1, *P1, sl 1 purlwise*. *Row 4:* *Sl 1 purlwise, P1, wyib*, P1. Rep these 4 rows. While knitting band, make four 2-st button-holes on the 2nd row of the right front, making the 1st buttonhole (3) 2 [3] sts from the edge and the rem at intervals of (11) 14 [16] sts. BO in patt.

Sew a pocket onto the center of each front 1"/2.5cm from the bottom edge.

Sew the buttons on left front.

Pants ★

Sizes

(3 months) 6 months [12 months]

Materials

Any pure wool light worsted weight yarn, such as Phildar's *Pure Laine* (100% wool; 1¾oz/50g = 118yd/108m) in colors: B (green–*Romarin/304*) and E (camel–*Chameau/306*)
Any acrylic-and-lamb's wool-blend fingering weight yarn, such as Phildar's *Super Baby* (70% acrylic/30% lamb's wool; ⅞oz/25g = 117yd/107m) in colors: C (dusky pink–*Bruyère/112*), F (rose pink–*Azalée/103*), and G (taupe–*Renne/123*)
Any wool-and-acrylic-blend sport weight yarn, such as Phildar's *Phil'Laine* (51% wool/49% acrylic; 1¾oz/50g = 138yd/126m) in D (gold–*Maïs/055*)
3 months: 3 balls B and a small amount of the other 5 colors
6 months: 4 balls B and a small amount of the other 5 colors
12 months: 5 balls B and a small amount of the other 5 colors
1 pair each #3/3mm and #4/3.5mm knitting needles, or sizes needed to obtain gauge
1 spare needle or stitch holder

Stitches

Stockinette Stitch: See hooded jacket instructions.
Moss Slip Stitch: See hooded jacket instructions.
Left-slanting decrease (SKP): See hooded jacket instructions.
Single Rib: *K1, P1*, rep from * to *.
To increase: Knit 1 st in the back of the st in the row below, then knit the st above as usual.

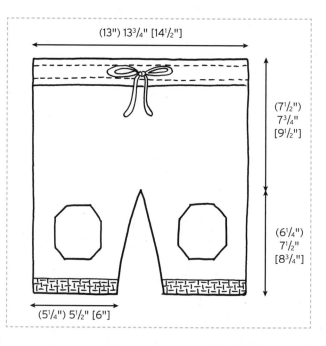

(13") 13¾" [14½"]

(7½") 7¾" [9½"]

(6¼") 7½" [8¾"]

(5¼") 5½" [6"]

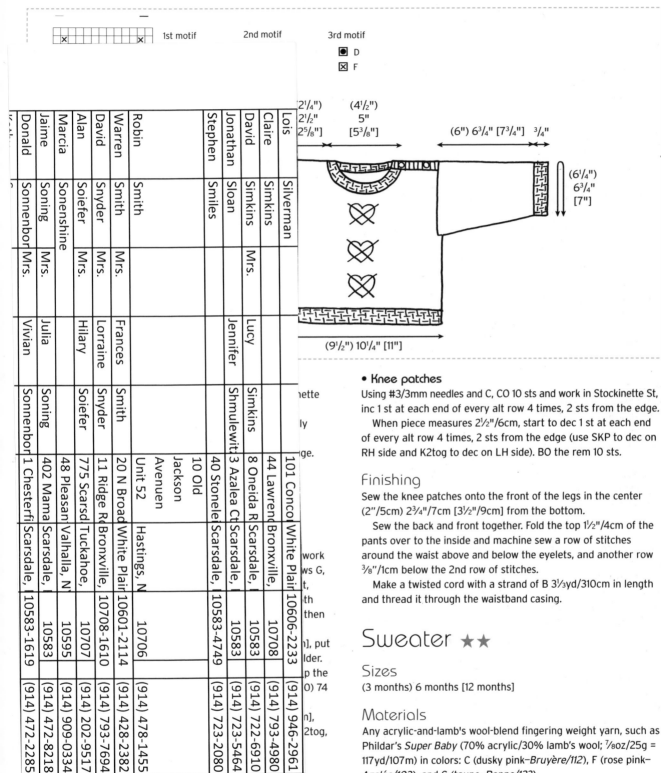

1st motif   2nd motif   3rd motif

● D
⊠ F

First name	Last name	Title	Name	Surname	Address	City	Zip	Phone
Lois	Silverman				101 Conco	White Plain	10606-2233	(914) 946-2961
Claire	Simkins				44 Lawren	Bronxville,	10708	(914) 793-4980
David	Simkins	Mrs.			8 Oneida R	Scarsdale,	10583	(914) 722-6910
Jonathan	Sloan		Lucy	Simkins	3 Azalea Ct	Scarsdale,	10583	(914) 723-5464
Stephen	Smiles		Jennifer	Shmulewit	40 Stonele	Scarsdale,	10583-4749	(914) 723-2080
Robin	Smith				10 Old Jackson Avenuen Unit 52	Hastings, N	10706	(914) 478-1455
Warren	Smith	Mrs.	Frances	Smith	20 N Broad	White Plain	10601-2114	(914) 428-2382
David	Snyder	Mrs.	Lorraine	Snyder	11 Ridge Rd	Bronxville,	10708-1610	(914) 793-7694
Alan	Soiefer	Mrs.	Hilary	Soiefer	775 Scarsd	Tuckahoe,	10707	(914) 202-9517
Marcia	Sonenshine				48 Pleasan	Valhalla, N	10595	(914) 909-0334
Jaime	Soning	Mrs.	Julia	Soning	402 Mama	Scarsdale,	10583	(914) 472-8218
Donald	Sonnenbor	Mrs.	Vivian	Sonnenbor	1 Chesterfi	Scarsdale,	10583-1619	(914) 472-2285

• Knee patches

Using #3/3mm needles and C, CO 10 sts and work in Stockinette St, inc 1 st at each end of every alt row 4 times, 2 sts from the edge.

When piece measures 2½"/6cm, start to dec 1 st at each end of every alt row 4 times, 2 sts from the edge (use SKP to dec on RH side and K2tog to dec on LH side). BO the rem 10 sts.

Finishing

Sew the knee patches onto the front of the legs in the center (2"/5cm) 2¾"/7cm [3½"/9cm] from the bottom.

Sew the back and front together. Fold the top 1½"/4cm of the pants over to the inside and machine sew a row of stitches around the waist above and below the eyelets, and another row ⅜"/1cm below the 2nd row of stitches.

Make a twisted cord with a strand of B 3⅓yd/310cm in length and thread it through the waistband casing.

Sweater ★★

Sizes

(3 months) 6 months [12 months]

Materials

Any acrylic-and-lamb's wool-blend fingering weight yarn, such as Phildar's *Super Baby* (70% acrylic/30% lamb's wool; ⅞oz/25g = 117yd/107m) in colors: C (dusky pink–*Bruyère/112*), F (rose pink–*Azalée/103*), and G (taupe–*Renne/123*)

Any pure wool light worsted weight yarn, such as Phildar's *Pure Laine* (100% wool; 1¾oz/50g = 118yd/108m) in colors: B (green–*Romarin/304*) and E (camel–*Chameau/306*)

Any wool-and-acrylic-blend sport weight yarn, such as Phildar's *Phil'Laine* (51% wool/49% acrylic; 1¾oz/50g = 138yd/126m) in D (gold–*Maïs/055*)

3 months: 4 balls C and a small amount of the other 5 colors
6 months: 4 balls C and a small amount of the other 5 colors
12 months: 6 balls C and a small amount of the other 5 colors
2 small pink 4-hole buttons
1 round-tipped embroidery needle
1 pair #3/3mm knitting needles, or size needed to obtain gauge
1 spare needle or stitch holder

Stitches

Stockinette Stitch: See hooded jacket instructions.
Seed Stitch: See hooded jacket instructions.

Embroidery Stitches

Heart motifs: Embroider in Duplicate Stitch over each Stockinette St, following the line of the original yarn, as shown in the chart.

Gauge

28 stitches and 37 rows to a 4"/10cm square knit in Stockinette St with yarn C on #3/3mm needles.

Take the time to make a gauge swatch, which is especially important if you are substituting the suggested yarn.
If necessary, change needle sizes to obtain the correct gauge.

Making the sweater

• Back

Using #3/3mm needles and C, CO (67) 73 [79] sts and work ¾"/2cm in Seed St, then cont even in Stockinette St.

When piece measures (5¼"/13cm) 6"/15cm [6¾"/17cm], beg shaping armholes: BO 2 sts at end of next 2 rows.**

Work even until piece measures (9"/23cm) 10¼"/26cm [11½"/29cm], then beg shaping neck: BO (17) 19 [23] sts in the center of the next row and cont working the sts on LH side.

On alt rows, beg at neck edge, BO 8 sts once, then cont even on the rem (15) 17 [18] sts.

When piece measures (9½"/24cm) 10¾"/27cm [11¾"/30cm], put the rem (15) 17 [18] sts on a spare needle or stitch holder.

Pick up and K the sts on RH side of the neck and work as LH side, reversing shapings, but BO the rem sts.

• Front

Work as for back to **.

Work even until piece measures (7½"/19cm) 8¾"/22cm [9¾"/25cm], then beg shaping neck: BO (11) 13 [17] sts in the center of the next row and cont working the sts on LH side. On alt rows, beg at neck edge, BO 3 sts twice, 2 sts once, and 1 st 3 times.

Work even until piece measures (9½"/24cm) 10¾"/27cm [11¾"/30cm], then BO the rem (15) 17 [18] sts. Pick up and K the sts on RH side and work as for LH side, reversing shapings.

When piece measures (9½"/24cm) 10¾"/27cm [11¾"/30cm], put the rem (15) 17 [18] sts on a spare needle or stitch holder.

• Sleeves

Using #3/3mm needles and C, CO (45) 48 [50] sts and work ¾"/2cm in Seed St, then cont in Stockinette St, inc 1 st at each end of every 4th row 5 times and 1 st at each end of every 6th row (5 times) 6 times [8 times].

Work even until piece measures (6¾"/17cm) 7½"/19cm [8¾"/22cm] and BO the resulting (65) 70 [76] sts.

Finishing

Embroider 3 heart motifs in Duplicate St (see chart) in the center of the front, the 1st (1⅜"/3.5cm) 1½"/4cm [1¾"/4.5cm] from the bottom, and the others at intervals of (1"/2.5cm) 1⅜"/3.5cm [1¾"/4.5cm]. Sew the right shoulder.

Using #3/3mm needles and C, pick up and K (70) 76 [82] sts evenly around the neck and work ¾"/2cm in Seed St. BO in patt.

Using #3/3mm needles and C, pick up and K 6 sts evenly along the edge of the back neckband, then pick up the sts at the shoulder and work ⅝"/1.5cm in Single Rib. BO in rib.

Work the front shoulder to match, making two 2-st buttonholes, the 1st buttonhole (6) 6 [7] sts from the edge and the 2nd after another (8) 9 [10] sts. BO in rib.

Fit the shoulder edges together and sew at the armhole edge.

Fit and sew the sleeves and sides of the sweater.

Sew on the buttons in line with the buttonholes.

Beret ★★

Size
12 months

Materials
Any wool-and-acrylic-blend sport weight yarn, such as Phildar's *Phil'Laine* (51% wool/49% acrylic; 1¾oz/50g = 138yd/126m) in D (gold–*Maïs/055*)
Any acrylic-and-lamb's wool-blend fingering weight yarn, such as Phildar's *Super Baby* (70% acrylic/30% lamb's wool; ⅞oz/25g = 117yd/107m) in colors: C (dusky pink–*Bruyère/112*), F (rose pink–*Azalée/103*), and G (taupe–*Renne/123*)
Any pure wool light worsted weight yarn, such as Phildar's *Pure Laine* (100% wool; 1¾oz/50g = 118yd/108m) in colors: B (green–*Romarin/304*) and E (camel–*Chameau/306*)
Quantity: 1 ball D and a small amount of the other 5 colors
1 pair #4/3.5mm knitting needles, or size needed to obtain gauge
5 #4/3.5mm double-pointed needles, or size needed to obtain gauge

Stitches
Circular Stockinette Stitch: Work all rows in K.
Moss Slip Stitch: See hooded jacket instructions.
To increase: K 1 st in the back of the st in the row below, then K the st above as usual.
Double decrease (dble dec): Sl 2 tog knitwise, K1, PSSO.

Gauge
23 stitches and 30 rows to a 4"/10cm square knit in Stockinette St with yarn D on #4/3.5mm needles.

Take the time to make a gauge swatch, which is especially important if you are substituting the suggested yarn.
If necessary, change needle sizes to obtain the correct gauge.

Making the beret
Using #4/3.5mm needles and B, CO 110 sts and work 16 rows in Moss Slip St, alternating 2 rows C, 2 rows D, 2 rows G, 2 rows E, 2 rows F, 2 rows B, 2 rows C, and 2 rows G, BO 1 st at beg of last 2 rows. Divide the sts evenly between 4 dpn and cont in D in Circular Stockinette St, turning the piece and inc 12 sts evenly on 1st row as foll: K9, *inc 1 st, K1, inc 1 st, K17*, rep from * to * 5 times, then inc 1 st, K1, inc 1 st, K8. Rep these incs on the next 4 rows. On the resulting 132 sts work even for 4 rows, then beg to dec as foll: K10, *1 dble dec, K19*, rep from * to * 5 times, then K9. Rep these decs every 4th row twice, every 3rd row 3 times, and every alt row 4 times. On foll row knit the sts tog in pairs, then cut the yarn, pass it through the rem 6 sts, and pull up to close.

Sew the edge of the beret.

Make a small pompom in F, 1¼"/3cm in diameter, and sew it to the top of the beret.

Booties ★★

Sizes
3 months (6 months)

Materials
Any acrylic-and-lamb's wool-blend fingering weight yarn, such as Phildar's *Super Baby* (70% acrylic/30% lamb's wool; ⅞oz/25g = 117yd/107m) in colors: C (dusky pink–*Bruyère/112*), F (rose pink–*Azalée/103*), and G (taupe–*Renne/123*)
Any wool-and-acrylic-blend sport weight yarn, such as Phildar's *Phil'Laine* (51% wool/49% acrylic; 1¾oz /50g = 138yd/126m) in D (gold–*Maïs/055*)
Any pure wool light worsted weight yarn, such as Phildar's *Pure Laine* (100% wool; 1¾oz/50g = 118yd/108m) in colors: B (green–*Romarin/304*) and E (camel–*Chameau/306*)
3 months: ½oz/15g G and a small amount of the other 5 colors
6 months: ¾oz/20g G and a small amount of the other 5 colors
1 pair #3/3mm knitting needles, or size needed to obtain gauge
2 spare needles

Stitches
Stockinette Stitch: See hooded jacket instructions.
Seed Stitch: See hooded jacket instructions.
Moss Slip Stitch: See hooded jacket instructions.

Gauge
See sweater instructions.

Making the booties
Using #3/3mm needles and B, CO 38 (44) sts and work 14 rows in Moss Slip St, alternating 2 rows C, 2 rows D, 2 rows G, 2 rows E, 2 rows F, 2 rows B, and 2 rows G, at the same time inc 1 st at each end and at either side of the 2 center sts, every alt row 5 times.

On the resulting 58 (64) sts, cont even in G in Stockinette St. Work 18 (20) rows, then cut the yarn. Place the 23 (25) sts at either end on spare needles and cont working only on the 12 (14) sts in the center to make the upper part of the bootie. K *11 (13), sl 1, knit the 1st of the reserved sts, PSSO, turn*, rep from * to * until only 16 (18) sts rem on either side. Cut the yarn. Pick up the 16 (18) sts on RH side, the 12 (14) sts from the upper part of the bootie, and finally the 16 (18) sts rem on LH side. Work ¾"/2cm in Stockinette St, then ⅜"/1cm in Seed St. BO in patt.

Work 2nd bootie to match 1st bootie.

Finishing
Weave in the tails, then close the sole and the back of the bootie.

Make 2 twisted cords with a strand of G 63"/160cm in length and thread one through the top edge of each bootie like a lace.

Make 4 small pompoms in F and sew one to each end of the cords.

a touch of folklore

a touch of folklore

A striped wrap top and embroidered sweater teamed up with olive pants … very trendy!

Embroidered sweater ★★

Sizes
(3 months) 6 months [12 months]

Materials
Any acrylic-and-lamb's wool-blend fingering weight yarn, such as Phildar's *Super Baby* (70% acrylic/30% lamb's wool; ⅞oz/25g = 117yd/107m) in colors: A (ecru–*Écru/085*), B (rose pink–*Azalée/103*), C (apricot–*Mangue/104*), D (olive green–*Olive/110*), and E (coral pink–*Grenadine/119*)
Any acrylic-and-wool-blend fingering weight yarn, such as Phildar's *Phil Luxe* (85% acrylic/15% wool; 1¾oz/50g = 220yd/201m) in colors: F (red–*Rouge/018*) and G (cerise–*Bengale/034*)
For all sizes: 4 balls of A and a small amount of the other colors
3 small pearl buttons
1 round-tipped embroidery needle
1 pair #3/3mm knitting needles, or size needed to obtain gauge

Stitches
Stockinette Stitch: K 1 row, P 1 row.
Garter Stitch: K every row.

Embroidery Stitches
Motifs: Embroidered in Cross-stitch, across 1 st and 1 row of work.

Gauges
30 stitches and 40 rows to a 4"/10cm square knit in Stockinette St with yarn A on #3/3mm needles.

30 stitches and 46 rows to a 4"/10cm square knit in Stockinette St and Garter Stitch with yarn A on #3/3mm needles.

Take the time to make a gauge swatch, which is especially important if you are substituting the suggested yarn.
If necessary, change needle sizes to obtain the correct gauge.

Making the embroidered sweater

• Back
Using #3/3mm needles and A, CO (68) 74 [80] sts and work 4 rows in Garter St.** Cont even in Stockinette St.

When piece measures (6"/15cm) 7"/18cm [8¼"/21cm], make the opening by BO the 2 sts in the center and cont working the sts on LH side.

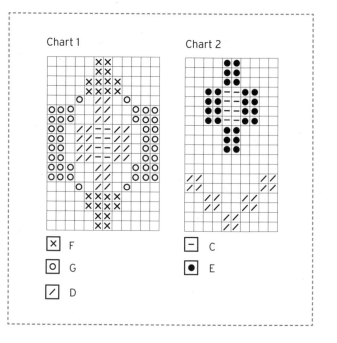

Chart 1

Chart 2

☒	F
⊙	G
⁄	D

| — | C |
| ⊙ | E |

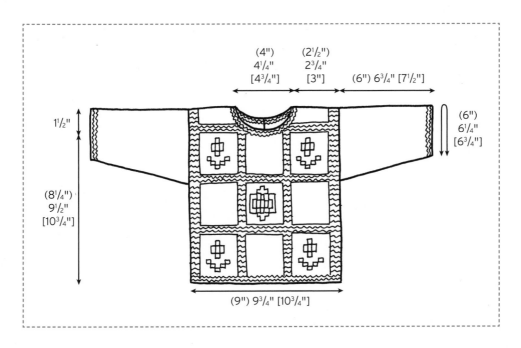

When piece measures (9½"/24cm) 10¾"/27cm [11¾"/30cm], beg shaping neck: On alt rows, beg at neck edge, BO (10) 11 [13] sts once and 4 sts once.

Work even until piece measures (9¾"/25cm) 11"/28cm [12¼"/31cm], then BO the rem (19) 21 [22] sts for the shoulder.

Pick up the sts on RH side and complete as for LH side, reversing shapings.

• Front
Work as for back to **.

Cont as foll: 4 sts in Garter St, *(18) 20 [22] sts in Stockinette St, 3 sts in Garter St*, rep from * to * twice, finishing with 4 sts in Garter St.

Work in this way for (26) 28 [30] rows, then work 6 complete rows in Garter St. Rep these (32) 34 [36] rows over the full length of the sweater front.

When piece measures (8¼"/21cm) 9½"/24cm [10¾"/27cm], beg shaping neck: BO (10) 12 [16] sts in the center of the next row and work each side separately. On alt rows, beg at neck edge, BO 3 sts once, 2 sts twice, and 1 st 3 times.

When piece measures (9¾"/25cm) 11"/28cm [12¼"/31cm], BO the rem (19) 21 [22] sts for the shoulder. Work other side to match, reversing shapings.

• Sleeves
Using #3/3mm needles and A, CO (46) 48 [50] sts and work 4 rows in Garter St, then cont even in Stockinette St, inc 1 st at each end of every 4th row (5) 7 [9] times, then every 6th row 5 times.

When piece measures (6"/15cm) 6¾"/17cm [7½"/19cm], BO the resulting (66) 72 [78] sts.

Finishing
Embroider the motifs on the front in the center of the squares of Stockinette Stitch: Motif #1 in the center square, then motif #2 in each corner square (see chart).

Sew the shoulder seams.

Using A, pick up and K (76) 84 [92] sts evenly around the neck. Work 4 rows in Garter St, then BO.

Using A, pick up and K 33 sts evenly along the LH edge of the back opening and knit 4 rows in Garter St, making three 2-st buttonholes on the 2nd row, the 1st buttonhole 4 sts from the edge and the others at 9-st intervals, then BO.

Work a similar border on the RH side of the opening, omitting the buttonholes.

Fit the buttonhole and button bands together and sew along the bottom edge.

Fit and close the sleeves.

Sew the side seams of the sweater.

Sew on the buttons in line with the buttonholes.

Pants ★

Sizes
(3 months) 6 months [12 months]

Materials
Any acrylic-and-lamb's wool-blend fingering weight yarn, such as Phildar's *Super Baby* (70% acrylic/30% lamb's wool; 7/8oz/25g = 117yd/107m) in D (olive green–*Olive/110*)

3 months: 4 balls
6 months: 4 balls
12 months: 6 balls
1 pair each #2/2.5mm and #3/3mm knitting needles, or sizes needed to obtain gauge
1 spare needle or stitch holder
elastic cording

Stitches
Single Rib: *K1, P1*, rep from * to *.
Stockinette Stitch: See embroidered sweater instructions.
Garter Stitch: See embroidered sweater instructions.
Left-slanting decrease (SKP): See embroidered sweater instructions.

Gauge
See embroidered sweater instructions.

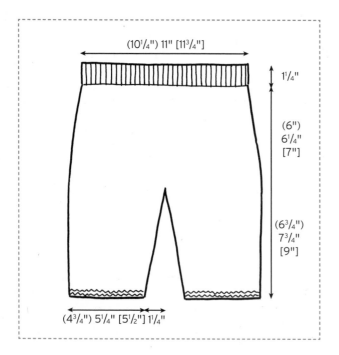

Making the pants

• Front
Begin with the right leg.

Using #3/3mm needles and D, CO (36) 39 [42] sts and work 4 rows in Garter St, then cont even in Stockinette St, inc 1 st on the RH side (every 6th row 9 times) every 6th and 8th row alternately 9 times [every 8th and 10th row alternately 9 times].

When piece measures (6¾"/17cm) 7¾"/20cm [9"/23cm], put the resulting (45) 48 [51] sts on a spare needle or stitch holder.

Work the left leg to match, reversing the shapings, then pick up and K the sts from the 1st leg and cont on the resulting (90) 96 [102] sts, dec 2 sts in the center as foll: K (43) 46 [49], K2tog, SKP, K (43) 46 [49] sts. Rep this every alt row 5 times, lining up the decs with those on the previous row.

When piece measures (12½"/32cm) 14¼"/36cm [16¼"/41cm], change to #2/2.5mm needles and work 1¼"/3cm in Single Rib, then BO in rib.

• Back
Work as for front.

Finishing
Sew the garment.

Thread a few strands of elastic cording through the waistband ribbing.

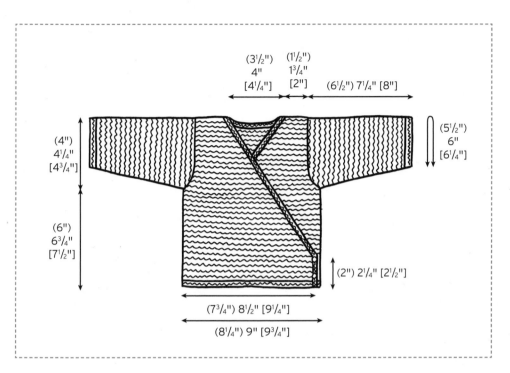

Wrap top ★★

Sizes
(3 months) 6 months [12 months]

Materials
Any acrylic-and-lamb's wool-blend fingering weight yarn, such as Phildar's *Super Baby* (70% acrylic/30% lamb's wool; ⁷/₈oz/25g = 117yd/107m) in colors: A (ecru–*Écru/085*), B (rose pink–*Azalée/103*), C (apricot–*Mangue/104*), D (olive green–*Olive/110*), and E (coral pink–*Grenadine/119*)
Any acrylic-and-wool-blend fingering weight yarn, such as Phildar's *Phil Luxe* (85% acrylic/15% wool; 1³/₄oz/50g = 220yd/201m) in colors: F (red–*Rouge/018*) and G (cerise–*Bengale/034*)
For all sizes: 2 balls A, B, C, D, and E, 1 ball F and G
3 small pearl buttons
1 pair each #2/2.5mm and #3/3mm knitting needles, or sizes needed to obtain gauge

Stitches
Garter Stitch: See embroidered sweater instructions.
Striped Garter Stitch: K *2 rows D, 2 rows F, 2 rows E, 2 rows D, 2 rows C, 2 rows E, 2 rows D, 2 rows G, 2 rows C, 2 rows G*, rep from * to *.

Gauge
28 stitches and 58 rows to a 4"/10cm square knit in Garter St on #3/3mm needles.

Take the time to make a gauge swatch, which is especially important if you are substituting the suggested yarn. If necessary, change needle sizes to obtain the correct gauge.

Making the wrap top

• Back
Using #2/2.5mm needles and A, CO (58) 64 [70] sts and work 4 rows in Garter St, then change to #3/3mm needles and cont even in Striped Garter St.

When piece measures (6"/15cm) 6³/₄"/17cm [7½"/19cm], beg shaping armholes: On alt rows, beg at armhole edge, dec 3 sts once and 1 st (2) 2 [3] times.

When piece measures (9½"/24cm) 10³/₄"/27cm [11³/₄"/30cm], beg shaping neck: BO (26) 30 [32] sts in the center of the next row and complete each side separately.

Cont even until piece measures (9³/₄"/25cm) 11"/28cm [12¼"/31cm], BO the rem (11) 13 [14] sts for the shoulder.

Work other side of neck to match, reversing shapings.

• Left front
Using #2/2.5mm needles and A, CO (54) 60 [66] sts and work 4 rows in Garter St. Change to #3/3mm needles and cont even in Striped Garter St.

When piece measures (2"/5cm) 2¼"/5.5cm [2½" 6cm], beg shaping diagonal neckline. Beg at neck edge, dec *1 st every alt row once, then 1 st every 4th row once*, rep from * to * (17) 20

[23] times altogether, then dec 1 st every 2nd row (4) 2 [0] times. When piece measures (6"/15cm) 6¾"/17cm [7½"/19cm], beg shaping armholes: On alt rows, beg at armhole edge, dec 3 sts once and 1 st (2) 2 [3] times.

When piece measures (9¾"/25cm) 11"/28cm [12¼"/31cm], BO the rem (11) 13 [14] sts for the shoulder.

• Right front

Work as for left front, reversing shapings.

• Sleeves

Using #2/2.5mm needles and A, CO (39) 42 [45] sts and work 4 rows in Garter St. Change to #3/3mm needles and cont in Striped Garter St, inc 1 st at each end of (every 8th row 9 times) every 6th row 5 times, then every 8th row 5 times [every 8th row 11 times].

When piece measures (6"/15cm) 6¾"/17cm [7½"/19cm], dec 2 sts at each end every alt row once and 1 st at each end every alt row 3 times, then BO the rem (47) 52 [57] sts.

Finishing

Sew the shoulders.

Using #2/2.5mm needles and A, pick up and K (15) 16 [18] sts evenly along the edge of the right front, then (60) 68 [75] sts along the diagonal edge, (26) 30 [32] sts along the back neck, (60) 68 [75] sts along the left front diagonal edge, and (15) 16 [18] sts along the left front edge. On the resulting (176) 198 [218] sts, work 4 rows in Garter St, making three 2-st buttonholes

on the 2nd row, the 1st buttonhole 4 sts from the RH edge, the 2nd at an interval of 6 sts, and the 3rd 4 sts from the LH edge. BO.

Fit and sew the sleeves and the sides of the top.

Sew on the buttons in line with the buttonholes, crossing the right front over the left front.

Pixie hat ★

Sizes
(3 months) 6 months [12 months]

Materials
Any acrylic-and-lamb's wool-blend fingering weight yarn, such as Phildar's *Super Baby* (70% acrylic/30% lamb's wool; ⅞oz/25g = 117yd/107m) in colors: A (ecru–*Écru/085*), C (apricot–*Mangue/104*), D (olive green–*Olive/110*), and E (coral pink–*Grenadine/119*)
For all sizes: 2 balls D, ⅓oz/10g A, and a small amount of each of the other 3 colors
1 pair each #2/2.5mm and #3/3mm knitting needles, or sizes needed to obtain gauge
1 round-tipped embroidery needle

Stitches
Stockinette Stitch: See embroidered sweater instructions.
Garter Stitch: See embroidered sweater instructions.
Left-slanting decrease (SKP): See embroidered sweater instructions.
Motif: Embroidered in Cross-stitch, across 1 st and 1 row of work.

Gauge
See embroidered sweater instructions.

Making the pixie hat

• Hat

Using #2/2.5mm needles and A, CO (105) 117 [126] sts and work 4 rows in Garter St. Change to #3/3mm needles and D and cont even in Stockinette St.

When piece measures (5½"/14cm) 6"/15cm [6¼"/16cm], *dec 1 st at each end of next row, then work 1 row. Dec 2 sts at each end of next row, then work 1 row*. Rep from * to * (14) 16 [17] more times, then dec 1 st each end of next row and BO rem (13) 13 [16] sts.

• Earflaps

Using #3/3mm needles and A, CO 20 sts and work even in Stockinette St.

Beg on the 13th row, dec 1 st at each end of every 2nd row 5 times, making dec 1 st in from the edge (use K2tog to dec on RH side and SKP to dec on LH side). BO the rem 10 sts.

Using #2/2.5mm needles and A, pick up and K 42 sts evenly around the edge of the earflaps and work 2 rows in Garter St, then BO.

Finishing

Embroider motif #2 (see chart) from the sweater in the center of each earflap, beg at the top of the Garter St edging.

Sew the hat, then sew the earflaps onto the inside (2"/5cm) 2¾"/7cm [3½"/8.5cm] from the seam.

Make 2 twisted cords in A, 9"/23cm in length, and sew them to the earflaps.

Make a pompom about 2"/5cm in diameter using all the colors (use any spare pieces of yarn left over from the other garments), and sew it onto the point of the hat.

Booties ★★

Sizes
3 months (6 months)

Materials
Any acrylic-and-lamb's wool-blend fingering weight yarn, such as Phildar's *Super Baby* (70% acrylic/30% lamb's wool; ⅞oz/25g = 117yd/107m) in colors: A (ecru–*Écru/085*), B (rose pink–*Azalée/103*), C (apricot–*Mangue/104*), D (olive green–*Olive/110*), and E (coral pink–*Grenadine/119*)
Any acrylic-and-wool-blend fingering weight yarn, such as Phildar's *Phil Luxe* (85% acrylic/15% wool; 1¾oz/50g = 220yd/201m) in colors: F (red–*Rouge/018*) and G (cerise–*Bengale/034*)
For both sizes: A small amount of each of the colors
1 pair #3/3mm knitting needles, or size needed to obtain gauge
2 spare needles or stitch holders

Stitches
Garter Stitch: See embroidered sweater instructions.
Striped Garter Stitch: See wrap top instructions.

Gauge
See wrap top instructions.

Making the booties
Begin with the sole.

Using #3/3mm needles and D, CO 11 (13) sts and work even in Striped Garter St.

When piece measures 3"/7.5cm (3¼"/8cm), CO another 23 (25) sts at each end and cont even on all sts. Work 18 (20) rows,

then cut the yarn. Leave the 23 (25) sts at either end on a spare needle or stitch holder and work only on the center 11 (13) sts to make the upper part of the bootie. K *10 (12), sl 1, K the 1st of the reserved sts and PSSO, turn*, rep from * to * until only 13 (15) sts rem in reserve on either side. Cut the yarn. Pick up and K the 13 (15) sts on the RH side, then the 11 (13) sts from the upper part of the bootie, and finally the 13 (15) sts on LH side. Work 22 (26) rows even in Striped Garter St, then 4 rows in A, and BO.

Finishing
Weave in the tails, then stitch the sides of the bootie to the sole and sew the seam.

Make a 2nd bootie to match the 1st bootie.

black and white

Teamed up with overalls in all-over cable knit, the embroidered Jacquard Stitch delicately accentuates the contrast of the negative against the positive.

Overalls ★★

Sizes
(6 months) 12 months [18 months]

Materials
Any wool-and-cashmere-blend sport weight yarn, such as Phildar's *Laine et cachemire* (85% combed wool/15% cashmere; $7/8$oz/25g = 66yd/60m) in black (*Noir/067*)
6 months: 7 balls
12 months: 9 balls
18 months: 10 balls
(5) 5 [6] small white 4-hole buttons
1 cable needle
1 pair each #4/3.5mm and #6/4mm knitting needles, or sizes needed to obtain gauge
1 spare needle or stitch holder

Stitches
Single Rib: *K1, P1*, rep from * to *.
Cable Rib: Cables cover 10 stitches across the chart.
4 stitches crossed to the right: Sl 2 sts onto the cn and place it behind the work, K the next 2 sts, then K the 2 sts on the cn.

Gauge
28 stitches and 30 rows to a 4"/10cm square knit in slightly loose Cable Rib on #6/4mm needles.

Take the time to make a gauge swatch, which is especially important if you are substituting the suggested yarn. If necessary, change needle sizes to obtain the correct gauge.

Making the overalls
The overalls are knit in one piece, beg with the left leg.

Using #6/4mm needles, CO (56) 61 [67] sts and work in Cable Rib beg at (a) b [a] on the chart, and inc 1 st at each end of every (14th) 18th [22nd] row 3 times. After the last row of the patt, beg again with the 3rd row.

When piece measures (6¾"/17cm) 8¼"/21cm [9¾"/25cm], put the (62) 67 [73] resulting sts on a spare needle or stitch holder.

Work the right leg in the same way, beg at (a) a [c] on the chart.

When piece measures (6¾"/17cm) 8¼"/21cm [9¾"/25cm], CO 7 sts onto a spare needle, then pick up the sts from the right leg, CO 18 sts for the crotch, pick up the sts from the left leg, and CO 7 more sts. Cont even in Cable Rib on resulting (156) 166 [178] sts.

When piece measures (13¾"/35cm) 16½"/42cm [19"/48cm], beg shaping armholes: K (35) 38 [41], BO 6 sts, K (74) 78 [84], BO 6 sts, and K (35) 38 [41]. Cont even on these sts for the left front.

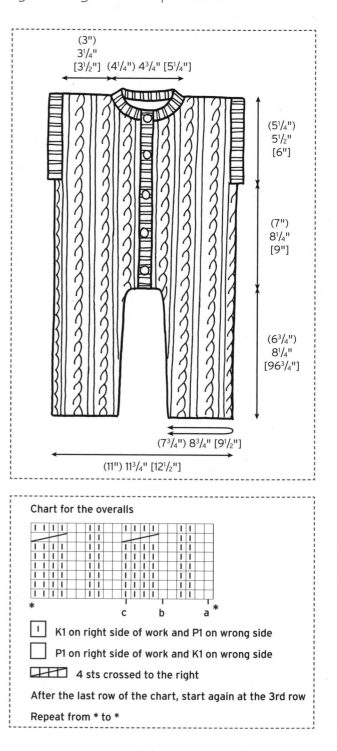

Chart for the overalls

	K1 on right side of work and P1 on wrong side
	P1 on right side of work and K1 on wrong side
	4 sts crossed to the right

After the last row of the chart, start again at the 3rd row

Repeat from * to *

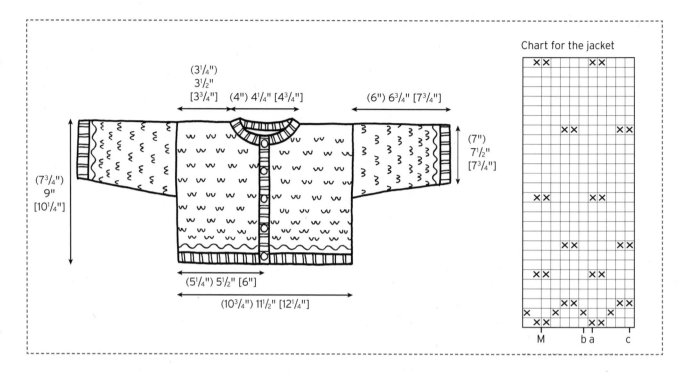

Chart for the jacket

When piece measures (17¼"/44cm) 20"/51cm [22¾"/58cm], beg shaping neck: On alt rows, beg at neck edge, BO (6) 7 [7] sts once, (4) 4 [5] sts once, (3) 4 [4] sts once, and 1 st once.

When piece measures (19"/48cm) 22"/56cm [24¾"/63cm], BO the rem (21) 22 [24] sts for the shoulder.

Pick up the (35) 38 [41] sts for the right front and complete it to match the left, reversing shapings.

Pick up the (74) 78 [84] sts for the back and cont even.

When piece measures (18½"/47cm) 21½"/55cm [24½"/62cm], beg shaping neck: BO (32) 34 [36] sts in the center of the next row and complete each side separately.

When piece measures (19"/48cm) 22"/56cm [24¾"/63cm], BO the rem (21) 22 [24] sts for the shoulder.

Work other side of neck to match.

Finishing

Make the same border for all the armhole edges: Pick up and K (31) 33 [34] sts evenly, work ¾"/2cm in Single Rib, then BO in rib.

Pick up and K (67) 75 [82] sts evenly along the right front and knit ⅝"/1.5cm in Single Rib, then BO in rib. Work the same border along the left front, making (4) 4 [5] 2-st buttonholes on the 2nd row, the 1st buttonhole (11) 12 [11] sts from the edge and the others at intervals of (13) 15 [13] sts.

Sew the shoulder seams.

Pick up and K (69) 75 [81] sts evenly around the neck and knit ⅝"/1.5cm in Single Rib, making a buttonhole 2 sts from the LH edge.

Sew the leg and crotch seams, placing the buttonhole band over the button band.

Sew on the buttons in line with the buttonholes.

Black cardigan ★★

Sizes
(6 months) 12 months [18 months]

Materials
Any wool-and-cashmere-blend sport weight yarn, such as Phildar's *Laine et cachemire* (85% combed wool/15% cashmere; ⅞oz/25g = 66yd/60m) in colors: A (black–*Noir/067*) and B (ecru–*Écru/032*)
6 months: 4 balls A and 2 balls B
12 months: 6 balls A and 2 balls B
18 months: 6 balls A and 2 balls B
(5) 5 [6] small white 4-hole buttons
1 pair each #4/3.5mm and #6/4mm knitting needles, or sizes needed to obtain gauge

Stitches
Single Rib: See overalls instructions.
Stockinette Stitch: K 1 row, P 1 row.
Jacquard Stockinette Stitch: Follow the chart, twisting yarns together at each color change. After the last row, beg again with the 1st row.

Gauge

22 stitches and 29 rows to a 4"/10cm square knit in Jacquard Stockinette Stitch on #6/4mm needles.

Take the time to make a gauge swatch, which is especially important if you are substituting the suggested yarn. If necessary, change needle sizes to obtain the correct gauge.

Making the black cardigan

• Back

Using #4/3.5mm needles and A, CO (60) 64 [68] sts and work ⅝"/1.5cm in Single Rib. Change to #6/4mm needles and cont in Jacquard Stockinette St, beg at (a) b [c] on the chart.

When piece measures (7½"/19cm) 8¾"/22cm [9¾"/25cm], beg shaping neck: BO (18) 20 [22] sts in the center of the next row and complete each side separately. On alt rows, beg at neck edge, dec 2 sts once, then work even until piece measures (7¾"/20cm) 9"/23cm [10¼"/26cm]. BO the rem (19) 20 [21] sts for the shoulder.

Work other side to match, reversing shapings.

• Right front

Using #4/3.5mm needles and A, CO (29) 31 [33] sts and work ⅝"/1.5cm in Single Rib. Change to #6/4mm needles and cont even in Jacquard Stockinette St, beg at c on the chart.

When piece measures (7"/18cm) 8¼"/21cm [9½"/24cm], beg shaping neck: On alt rows, beg at neck edge, BO 7 sts once, (2) 3 [4] sts once, and 1 st once.

When piece measures (7¾"/20cm) 9"/23cm [10¼"/26cm], BO the rem (19) 20 [21] sts for the shoulder.

• Left front

Work as for right front, reversing shapings.

• Sleeves

Using #4/3.5mm needles and A, CO (40) 42 [44] sts and work ⅝"/1.5cm in Single Rib. Change to #6/4mm needles and cont even in Jacquard Stockinette St, making sure that point M on the chart is in the center of the work, and inc 1 st at each end of (every 8th row twice, then every 10th row twice) every 8th row 5 times [every 6th row 4 times, then every 8th row 3 times].

When piece measures (6"/15cm) 6¾"/17cm [7¾"/20cm], BO the resulting (48) 52 [58] sts.

Finishing

Sew the shoulder seams.

Using #4/3.5mm needles and A, pick up and K (53) 59 [65] sts evenly around neck and work ⅝"/1.5cm in Single Rib. BO in rib.

Using #4/3.5mm needles and A, pick up and K (45) 53 [61] sts evenly along the left front and work ⅝"/1.5cm in Single Rib, making (5) 5 [6] single-st buttonholes on the 2nd row, the 1st buttonhole 2 sts from the edge and the others at intervals of (9) 11 [10] sts, then BO in rib.

Work the same border along the right front, omitting the buttonholes.

Fit and sew in the sleeves and sew the sides of the cardigan. Sew the buttons onto the right front, in line with the buttonholes.

White sweater ★★

Sizes

(6 months) 12 months [18 months]

Materials

Any wool-and-cashmere-blend sport weight yarn, such as Phildar's *Laine et cachemire* (85% combed wool/15% cashmere; ⅞oz/25g = 66yd/60m) in colors: A (black–*Noir/067*) and B (ecru–*Écru/032*)
6 months: 4 balls B and 2 balls A
12 months: 6 balls B and 2 balls A
18 months: 6 balls B and 2 balls A
(5) 5 [6] small white 4-hole buttons
1 pair each #4/3.5mm and #6/4mm knitting needles, or sizes needed to obtain gauge

Stitches

Single Rib: See overalls instructions.
Stockinette Stitch: See black cardigan instructions.

Embroidery Stitches
Jacquard Stitch: Embroider over each Stockinette St in Duplicate St, following the line of the original yarn, as shown in the chart.

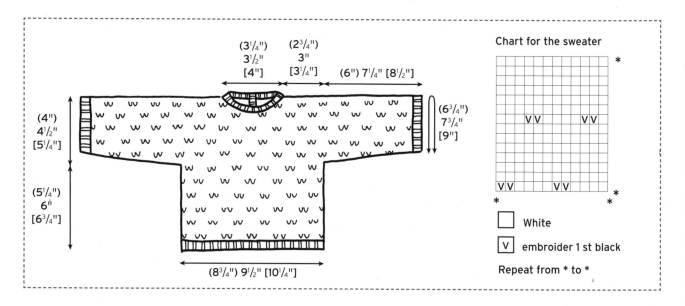

Chart for the sweater

☐ White

V embroider 1 st black

Repeat from * to *

Gauge

22 stitches and 29 rows to a 4"/10cm square knit in Stockinette St on #6/4mm needles.

Take the time to make a gauge swatch, which is especially important if you are substituting the suggested yarn. If necessary, change needle sizes to obtain the correct gauge.

Making the white sweater

The sweater is knit in one piece, beg with the front.

Using #4/3.5mm needles and B, CO (50) 54 [60] sts and work ⅝"/1.5cm in Single Rib, then change to #6/4mm needles and cont even in Stockinette St.

When piece measures (5¼"/13cm) 6"/15cm [6¾"/17cm], make the sleeves by inc at each end of every alt row (11 sts twice and 10 sts once) 13 sts 3 times [15 sts twice and 16 sts once]. Cont even on the resulting (114) 132 [152] sts.

When piece measures (8¼"/21cm) 9½"/24.5cm [11"/28cm], beg shaping neck: BO (12) 14 [16] sts in the center of the next row and cont working the (51) 59 [68] sts on LH side. On alt rows, beg at neck edge, dec 2 sts once and 1 st once.

When piece measures (9"/23cm) 10½"/26.5cm [11¾"/30cm] make a marker stitch to denote the position of the shoulder at the center point of the work.

Work another ⅜"/1cm, then beg shaping back neck: On alt rows, beg at neck edge, inc (4) 5 [5] sts once and (3) 3 [4] sts once. Cont even on the resulting (55) 64 [74] sts.

After working (3½"/8.5cm) 4"/10cm [4½"/11.5cm] from the shoulder marker stitch, complete the sleeve by BO on the left every alt row (11 sts twice and 10 sts once) 13 sts 3 times [15 sts twice and 16 sts once]. Cont even on the rem (23) 25 [28] sts.

After working (8½"/21.5cm) 9¾"/25cm [11¼"/28.5cm] from the shoulder marker stitch, change to #4/3.5mm needles and work ⅝"/1.5cm in Single Rib, then BO in rib.

Pick up the (51) 59 [68] sts held in reserve and complete the right side to match the left, reversing shapings.

Finishing

Embroider the front: beg on the 1st row of Stockinette St and work 2 sts in A in the center of the row. Embroider the back in reverse.

All the edgings are knit using #4/3.5mm needles.

Using B, pick up and K (45) 51 [61] sts evenly around the neck and work ⅝"/1.5cm in Single Rib, then BO in rib.

Pick up and K (55) 63 [71] sts evenly along the right back and work a matching border.

Work a matching border along the left back, but make (5) 5 [6] 2-st buttonholes on the 2nd row, the 1st buttonhole 2 sts from the edge and the others at intervals of (10) 12 [11] sts.

Using B, pick up and K (37) 39 [41] sts evenly along the bottom edge of the sleeves and work the same border.

Sew the sleeves and side seams.

Sew the buttons onto the RH side of the back, in line with the buttonholes.

adventurous babies

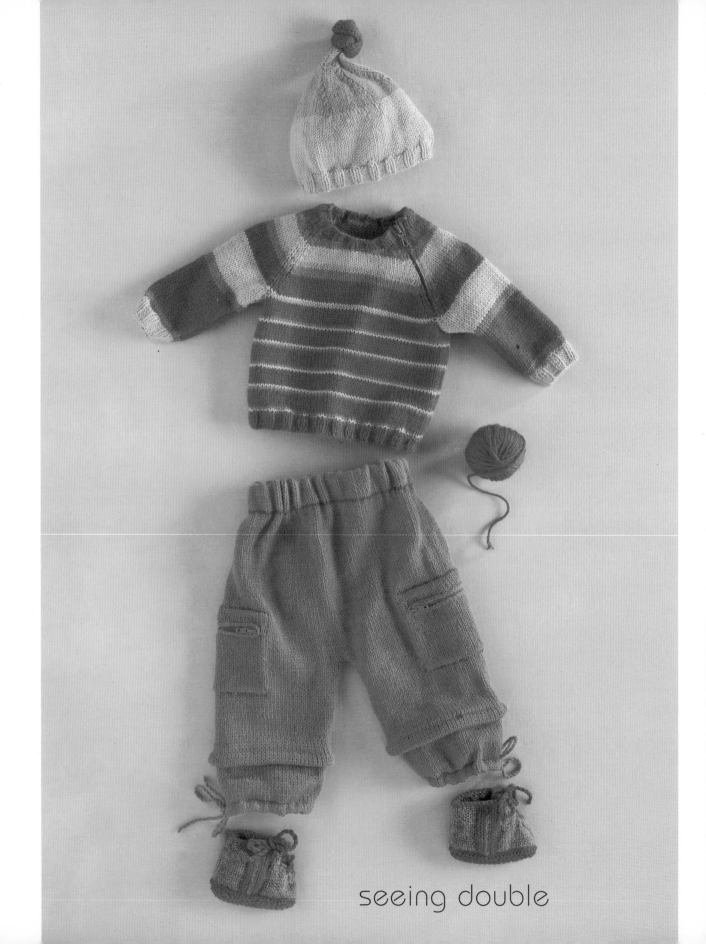

seeing double

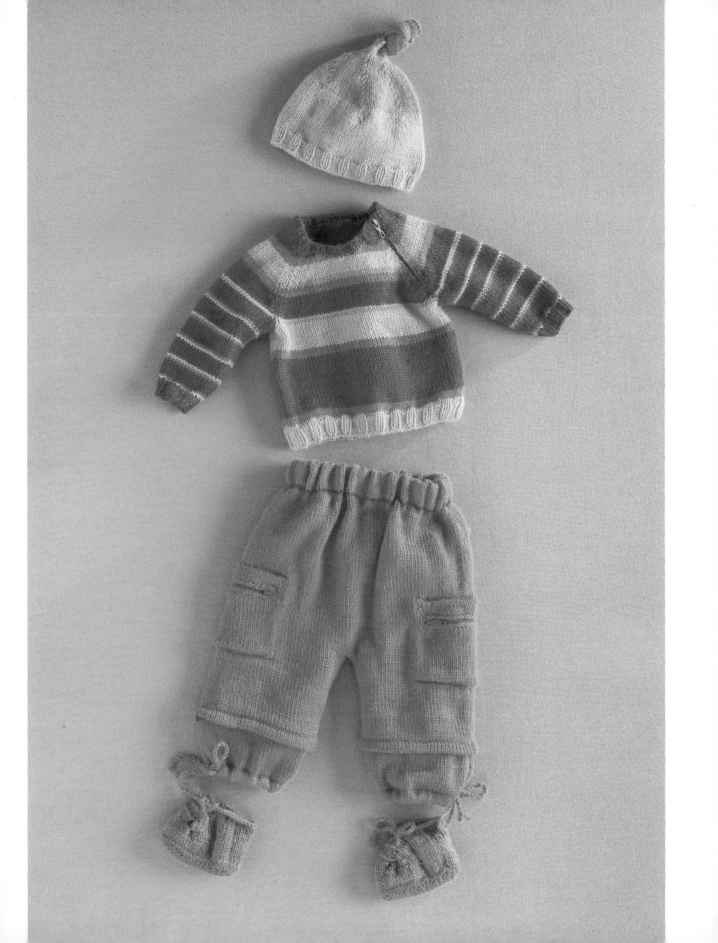

seeing double

Play a game of Who's Who? with these twin sweaters in reverse stripes.

Striped sweaters ★ ★ ★

Sizes
(3 months) 6 months [12 months]

Materials
Any lamb's wool-and-acrylic-blend fingering weight yarn, such as Phildar's *Lambswool* (51% lamb's wool/49% acrylic; 1¾oz/50g = 147yd/134m) in colors: A (fuchsia pink–*Fuchsia/004*), B (coral pink–*Freesia/020*), and C (candy pink–*Papaye/015*)
Any wool-and-acrylic-blend sport weight yarn, such as Phildar's *Phil'Laine* (51% wool/49% acrylic; 1¾oz /50g = 138yd/126m) in D (red–*Carmin/024*)
For all sizes: 1 ball of each color
1 4"/10cm red zipper
1 pair #3/3mm knitting needles, or size needed to obtain gauge

Stitches
K2/P3 Rib: *K2, P3*, rep from * to *.
Stockinette Stitch: K 1 row, P 1 row.
Striped Stockinette Stitch: *1 row B, 1 row A, 6 rows D, 1 row A, 1 row B, 6 rows D*, rep from * to *.
Left-slanting decrease (SKP): Sl 1 knitwise, K1, PSSO.

Gauge
26 stitches and 35 rows to a 4"/10cm square knit in Striped Stockinette St on #3/3mm needles.

Take the time to make a gauge swatch, which is especially important if you are substituting the suggested yarn.
If necessary, change needle sizes to obtain the correct gauge.

Making the sweater with narrow stripes

• Back
Using #3/3mm needles and D, CO (60) 65 [70] sts and work ⅝"/1.5cm in K2/P3 Rib, beg with K1, P3, then cont even in Striped Stockinette St.**

When piece measures (5¼"/13cm) 6"/15cm [7"/17.5cm], after the (5th) 6th [7th] stripe of D, while shaping raglans, work foll stripe patt: 1 row C, 1 row B, 8 rows D, (3) 4 [4] rows A, 2 rows C, (6) 6 [8] rows B, (3) 4 [4] rows A, and finish in D. For the raglans, BO 4 sts at beg of next 2 rows, then beg shaping: 2 sts in from the ends, dec 1 st from each end of (every alt row 16 times) every alt row 16 times, then every 4th row once [every alt row 17 times, then every 4th row once] (use K2tog to dec on RH side and SKP to dec on LH side).

When piece measures (9"/22.5cm) 10"/25.5cm [11½"/29cm], after the last dec for the raglan, BO the rem (20) 23 [26] sts at the neck.

• Front
Work as for back to **.

When piece measures (5¼"/13cm) 6"/15cm [7"/17.5cm], after the (5th) 6th [7th] stripe of D, cont in stripes as for back and beg raglans. BO 4 sts at beg of next 2 rows, then beg shaping: 2 sts in from the ends, dec 1 st from each end of (every alt row 13 times) every alt row 13 times, then every 4th row once [every alt row 14 times, then every 4th row once].

Work even until piece measures (7½"/19cm) 8¾"/22cm [10"/25.5cm], beg shaping neck: BO (10) 13 [14] sts in the center of the next row and complete each side separately. On alt rows, beg at neck edge, dec (4) 4 [5] sts once and 2 sts once.

When piece measures (8¼"/21cm) 9½"/24cm [11"/27.5cm], after the last dec for the raglan, BO the rem 2 sts.

• Right sleeve
Using #3/3mm needles and B, CO (34) 36 [39] sts and work ⅝"/1.5cm in K2/P3 Rib, beg with (P1) P2 [P1], K2, then cont in Stockinette St, inc 1 st at each end of (every 4th row 8 times) every 4th row 7 times, then every 6th row twice [every 4th row 7 times, then every 6th row 3 times]. At the same time, work the foll stripe patt: 2 rows B, (3) 4 [4] rows A, (20) 22 [26] rows D, (3) 4 [4] rows A, (10) 14 [16] rows B, 1 row C, 1 row B, 8 rows D,

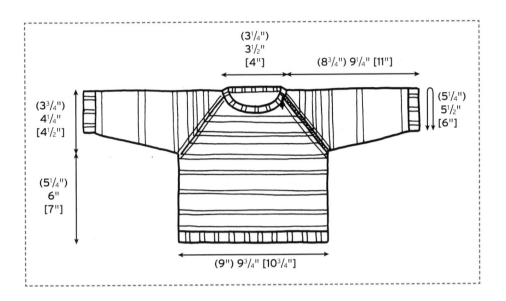

(3) 4 [4] rows A, 2 rows C, (6) 6 [8] rows B, (3) 4 [4] rows A, and finish in D.

When piece measures (5"/12.5cm) 5¾"/14.5cm [6½"/16.5cm], after (10) 14 [16] rows in B, beg shaping raglans. BO 4 sts at beg of next 2 rows, then shape the RH side dec as for the front, and shape the LH side dec as for the back. After the last dec for the front raglan, BO on RH side of every alt row, (4 sts twice and 5 sts once) 5 sts 3 times [6 sts 3 times].

• Left sleeve
Work as for right sleeve, reversing shapings.

Finishing
Fit the sleeves leaving the left front raglan open, and sew the sleeves and sides of the sweater. Pick up and K (68) 75 [83] sts evenly around the neck in D and knit ⅝"/1.5cm in K2/P3 Rib, beg with (P3) K1, P3 [P3], then BO in rib. Stitch the zipper into the raglan seam.

Making the sweater with broad stripes

• Back
Using #3/3mm needles and B, CO (60) 65 [70] sts and work ⅝"/1.5cm in K2/P3 Rib, beg with K1, P3, then cont even in Stockinette St, working foll stripe patt: 2 rows B, (3) 4 [4] rows A, (20) 22 [26] rows D, (3) 4 [4] rows A, (10) 14 [16] rows B, 1 row C, 1 row B, 8 rows D, (3) 4 [4] rows A, 2 rows C, (6) 6 [8] rows B, (3) 4 [4] rows A, and finishing in D.** At the same time, when piece measures (5¼"/13cm) 6"/15cm [7"/17.5cm], after (10) 14 [16] rows

in B, beg shaping raglans. BO 4 sts at beg of next 2 rows, then beg shaping: 2 sts in from the ends, dec 1 st at each end of (every alt row 16 times) every alt row 16 times, then every 4th row once [every alt row 17 times, then every 4th row once] (use K2tog to dec on RH side and SKP to dec on LH side).

When piece measures (9"/22.5cm) 10"/25.5cm [11½"/29cm], after the last dec for the raglan, BO the rem (20) 23 [26] sts at the neck.

• Front
Work as for back to **.

When piece measures (5¼"/13cm) 6"/15cm [7"/17.5cm], beg shaping raglans. BO 4 sts at beg of next 2 rows, then beg shaping: 2 sts in from the ends, dec 1 st at each end of (every alt row 13 times) 1 st every alt row 13 times, then every 4th row once [every alt row 14 times, then every 4th row once].

When piece measures (7½"/19cm) 8¾"/22cm [10"/25.5cm], beg shaping neck: BO (10) 13 [14] sts in the center of the next row and complete each side separately. On alt rows, beg at neck edge, BO (4) 4 [5] sts once and 2 sts once.

When piece measures (8¼"/21cm) 9½"/24cm [11"/27.5cm], after the last dec for the raglan, BO the rem 2 sts.

Work other side to match, reversing shapings.

• Right sleeve
Using #3/3mm needles and D, CO (34) 36 [39] sts and work ⅝"/1.5cm in K2/P3 Rib, beg with (P3) P2 [P1], K2, then cont in Striped Stockinette St, inc 1 st at each end of (every 4th row 8 times) every 4th row 7 times, then every 6th row twice [every 4th row 7 times, then every 6th row 3 times].

When piece measures (5"/12.5cm) 5¾"/14.5cm [6½"/16.5cm], after the (5th) 6th [7th] stripe of D, work foll stripe patt: 1 row C, 1 row B, 8 rows D, (3) 4 [4] rows A, 2 rows C, (6) 6 [8] rows B, (3) 4 [4] rows A, and finish with D. At the same time shape raglans: BO 4 sts at beg of next 2 rows, then shape the RH side of the dec as for front, and shape the LH side dec as for back. After the last dec for the front raglan, BO on RH side of every alt row (4 sts twice, then 5 sts once) 5 sts 3 times [6 sts 3 times].

• Left sleeve
Work as for right sleeve, reversing shapings.

Finishing
See sweater with narrow stripes.

Pants ★★★

Sizes
(3 months) 6 months [12 months]

Materials
Any lamb's wool-and-acrylic-blend fingering weight yarn, such as Phildar's *Lambswool* (51% lamb's wool/49% acrylic; 1¾oz/50g = 147yd/134m) in A (fuchsia pink–*Fuchsia/004*)
Any wool-and-acrylic-blend sport weight yarn, such as Phildar's *Phil'Laine* (51% wool/49% acrylic; 1¾oz /50g = 138yd/126m) in D (red–*Carmin/024*)
3 months: 3 balls A and a small amount of D
6 months: 3 balls A and a small amount of D
12 months: 4 balls A and small amount of D
2 4"/10cm red zippers
(16"/40cm) 18"/45cm [20"/50cm] 1"/2.5cm wide elastic
1 pair #3/3mm knitting needles, or size needed to obtain gauge
1 spare needle or stitch holder

Stitches
Stockinette Stitch: See striped sweaters instructions.

Gauge
26 stitches and 35 rows to a 4"/10cm square knit in Stockinette St on #3/3mm needles.
Take the time to make a gauge swatch, which is especially important if you are substituting the suggested yarn.
If necessary, change needle sizes to obtain the correct gauge.

Making the pants

• Back
Begin with the left leg.
Using #3/3mm needles and A, CO (34) 36 [39] sts and work in Stockinette St, inc 1 st on RH side (every 10 rows 4 times) every 10 rows 4 times [every 16 rows 4 times]. When piece measures (2¾"/7cm) 3¼"/8cm [3½"/9cm], work 4 rows D, then 4 rows A, then work the fold row by taking 1 st from the LH needle and simultaneously picking up the corresponding st from the A row below the 1st row of D and knitting the 2 sts tog. Cont even in Stockinette St in A.
When piece measures (6¼"/16cm) 7½"/19cm [8¾"/22cm], put the resulting (38) 40 [43] sts on a spare needle or stitch holder.
Work the right leg as the left, reversing shapings, then pick up the sts from the left leg and cont even on the resulting (76) 80 [86] sts.
When piece measures (12½"/32cm) 14½"/37cm [16½"/42cm], work 1 row D, then 2½"/6cm A, then BO.

• Front
Work as for back.

• Pockets
Using #3/3mm needles and A, CO 28 sts and work even in Stockinette St.
When piece measures 2½"/6cm, make opening: K3, BO 22 sts, K3. Work 1 row on the last 3 sts and put them on a spare needle or stitch holder. Work 1 row in purl on rem 3 sts, then 1 row in knit, then CO 22 sts and pick up and knit the last 3 sts. Work 5/8"/1.5cm on all sts, then BO.
Pick up and K 22 sts evenly along the top of the opening and work 1 row, binding off the sts purlwise.
Make a 2nd pocket in the same way.
Sew a zipper into the opening of each pocket.

Finishing
Sew the pants.
Make a ⅜"/1cm hem at the bottom of the legs.
Make 2 twisted cords with a 71"/180cm length of A, and thread one cord through each of the hems in the legs, tying them at the outer edge.
Make a 1¼"/3cm hem around the top of the pants and insert the elastic through the waistband casing.
Sew a pocket onto each leg (4¾"/12cm) 5½"/14cm [6¼"/16cm] from the bottom and centered over the side seam.

Hat ★★

Sizes
(3 months) 6 months [12 months]

Materials
Any lamb's wool-and-acrylic-blend fingering weight yarn, such as Phildar's *Lambswool* (51% lamb's wool/49% acrylic; 1¾oz/50g = 147yd/134m) in colors: A (fuchsia pink–*Fuchsia/004*), B (coral pink–*Freesia/020*), and C (candy pink–*Papaye/015*)

Any wool-and-acrylic-blend sport weight yarn, such as Phildar's *Phil'Laine* (51% wool/49% acrylic; 1³⁄₄oz /50g = 138yd/126m) in D (red–*Carmin/024*)
For all 3 sizes: ³⁄₄oz/20g B and C, and ¹⁄₂oz/15g A or D
1 pair #3/3mm knitting needles, or size needed to obtain gauge

Stitches
Stockinette Stitch: See striped sweaters instructions.
K2/P3 Rib: See striped sweaters instructions.

Gauge
See pants instructions.

Making the hat
Using #3/3mm needles and C, CO (92) 102 [112] sts and work ⁵⁄₈"/1.5cm in K2/P3 Rib with 1 selvage st at each end, then cont even in Stockinette St.

When piece measures (2¹⁄₂"/6cm) 2³⁄₄"/7cm [3¹⁄₄"/8cm], beg to dec. K (1) 3 [2], *K2tog, K (13) 14 [16]*, rep from * to * 6 times altogether, then K (1) 3 [2]. Rep these decs every 4th row twice more, cont in B after the 1st dec row, then every alt row (8) 9 [11] times. Work ³⁄₄"/2cm even on rem (26) 30 [28] sts, then 4¹⁄₄"/11cm in A or D, and BO. Sew the hat and tie a knot in the top.

Booties ★★

Sizes
3 months (6 months)

Materials
Any lamb's wool-and-acrylic-blend fingering weight yarn, such as Phildar's *Lambswool* (51% lamb's wool/49% acrylic; 1³⁄₄oz/50g = 147yd/134m) in colors: A (fuchsia pink–*Fuchsia/004*) and B (coral pink–*Freesia/020*)
Any wool-and-acrylic-blend sport weight yarn, such as Phildar's *Phil'Laine* (51% wool/49% acrylic; 1³⁄₄oz /50g = 138yd/126m) in D (red–*Carmin/024*)
3 months: ¹⁄₃oz/10g of each color
6 months: ¹⁄₂oz/15g of each color
1 pair #3/3mm knitting needles, or size needed to obtain gauge
1 round-tipped embroidery needle

Stitches
Stockinette Stitch: See striped sweaters instructions.
Garter Stitch: K every row.
Double decrease (SK2P): Sl 1 knitwise, K2 tog, PSSO.

Embroidery Stitches
Stripes: Embroider over each Stockinette St in Duplicate Stitch, following the line of the original yarn.

Gauge
See pants instructions.

Making the booties
Begin with the sole.

Using #3/3mm needles and A or D, CO 6 (8) sts and work in Garter St, inc 1 st at each end of every alt row twice.

When piece measures 2¹⁄₂"/6cm (2³⁄₄"/7cm), dec 1 st at each end of every alt row twice, then BO rem 6 (8) sts.

For the foot: Using #3/3mm needles and A or D, CO 56 (62) sts and work 2 rows in Garter St, 2 rows in Stockinette St, then change to B and cont even in Stockinette St. Work ³⁄₄"/2cm (1"/2.5cm), then beg the upper part of the bootie. K21 (23), K3tog, change to A or D, K 8 (10), then change back to B and SK2P, then K21 (23). Rep these decs every alt row 4 (5) more times, always making them at either side of the 8 (10) contrast sts of the upper part of the bootie. 36 (38) sts remain. Knit 1 row in A or D, then BO, working knitwise over purl sts.

Using A or D, embroider 2 stripes 2 sts wide on each side, with 1 st spacing in between, beg 8 (9) sts from the edge.

Sew the bootie and stitch on the sole. Make a twisted cord with a 63"/160cm length of A or D, and lace up the bootie.

Make a 2nd bootie in the same way.

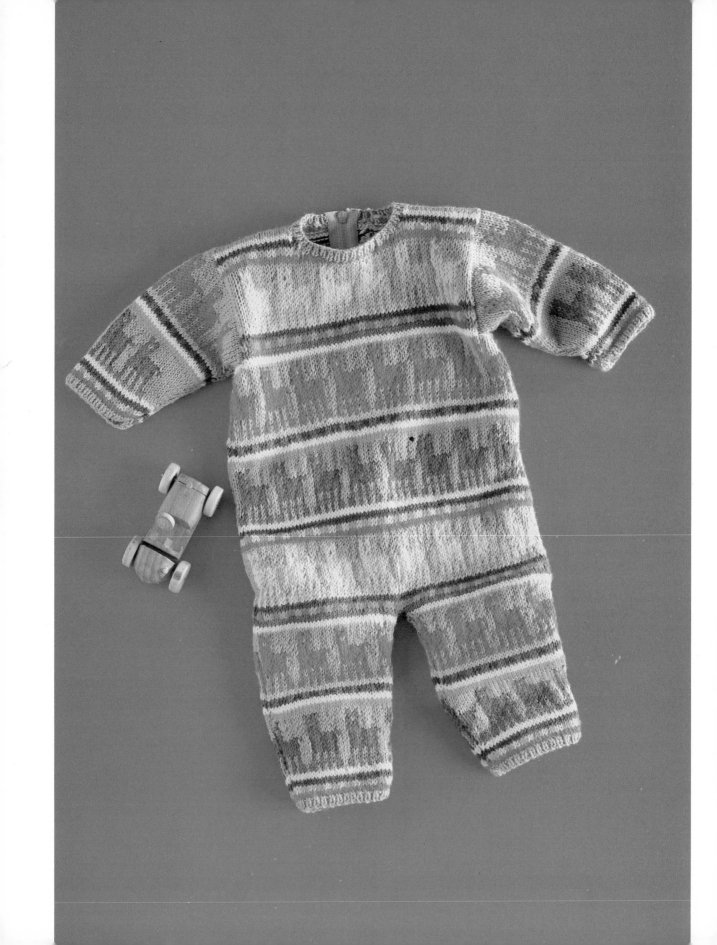

what a combination

what a combination

Choose rows of llamas or colorful stripes—the colors set the cheerful tone.

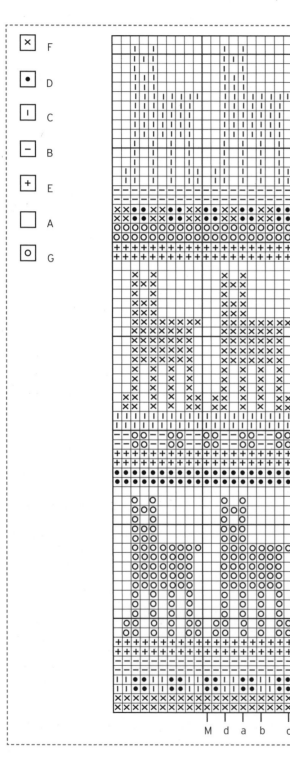

Llama romper ★★★

Sizes
(3 months) 6 months [12 months]

Materials
Any lamb's wool-and-acrylic-blend fingering weight yarn, such as Phildar's *Lambswool* (51% lamb's wool/49% acrylic; 1¾oz/50g = 147yd/134m) in colors: A (caramel–*Chanvre/080*), B (coffee–*Café/081*), C (lime green–*Perruche/093*), D (orange–*Curry/076*), E (yellow–*Canari/098*), F (fuchsia pink–*Fuchsia/004*), and G (jade–*Curaçao/002*)
3 months: 2 balls A and 1 ball each of the other 6 colors
6 months: 2 balls A and 1 ball each of the other 6 colors
12 months: 3 balls A and 1 ball each of the other 6 colors
1 (12"/30cm) 12"/30cm [14"/35cm] caramel-colored zipper
1 pair #3/3mm knitting needles, or size needed to obtain gauge
1 spare needle or stitch holder

Stitches
Single Rib: *K1, P1*, rep from * to *.
Stockinette Stitch: K 1 row, P 1 row.
Jacquard Stockinette Stitch: Follow the chart, twisting yarns together at each color change. After the last row, beg again with the 1st row.

Gauge
31 stitches and 33 rows to a 4"/10cm square knit in Jacquard Stockinette St on #3/3mm needles.

   Take the time to make a gauge swatch, which is especially important if you are substituting the suggested yarn. If necessary, change needle sizes to obtain the correct gauge.

Making the llama romper

• Front
Begin with right leg.
   Using #3/3mm needles and A, CO (31) 34 [37] sts and work ³⁄₈"/1cm in Single Rib, then cont in Jacquard Stockinette St, beg at a on the chart and inc 1 st at each end of (every 8th row twice, then every 10th row 3 times) every 10th row twice, then every 12th row 3 times [every 12th row twice, then every 14th row 3 times].
   When piece measures (6¾"/17cm) 7¾"/20cm [9"/23cm], put the resulting (41) 44 [47] sts on a spare needle or stitch holder.
   Work the 2nd leg in the same way, but beg the patt at (b) c [d] on the chart, then make 1 st and pick up the sts from the right leg. Cont even on the resulting (83) 89 [95] sts.

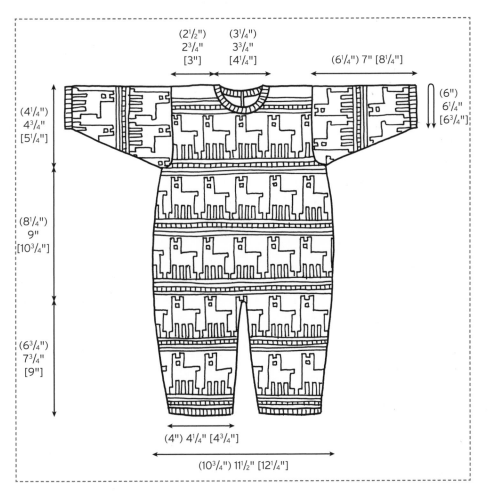

(2¹/₂")
2³/₄"
[3"]

(3¹/₄")
3³/₄"
[4¹/₄"]

(6¹/₄") 7" [8¹/₄"]

(6")
6¹/₄"
[6³/₄"]

(4¹/₄")
4³/₄"
[5¹/₄"]

(8¹/₄")
9"
[10³/₄"]

(6³/₄")
7³/₄"
[9"]

(4") 4¹/₄" [4³/₄"]

(10³/₄") 11¹/₂" [12¹/₄"]

When piece measures (12¹/₄"/31cm) 14¹/₄"/36cm [16¹/₄"/41cm], dec 1 st at each end of every 8th row 3 times.

When piece measures (15"/38cm) 17"/43cm [19³/₄"/50cm], beg shaping armholes: BO 5 sts at beg of next 2 rows, then cont even.

When piece measures (17³/₄"/45cm) 20"/51cm [23¹/₄"/59cm], beg shaping neck: BO (13) 15 [15] sts in the center of the next row and complete each side separately. On alt rows, beg at neck edge, BO 4 sts once, 2 sts (1) 1 [2] times, and 1 st once.

When piece measures (19¹/₄"/49cm) 21¹/₂"/55cm [24³/₄"/63cm], BO the rem (20) 22 [23] sts for the shoulder. Complete other side to match, reversing shapings.

• Left back
Using #3/3mm needles and A, CO (31) 34 [37] sts and work ³/₈"/1cm in Single Rib, then cont in Jacquard Stockinette St, beg at (b) c [d] on the chart and inc 1 st at each end of (every 8th row twice, then every 10th row 3 times) every 10th row

twice, then every 12th row 3 times [every 12th row twice, then every 14th row 3 times].

When piece measures (6³/₄"/17cm) 7³/₄"/20cm [9"/23cm], add 1 st on LH side, then cont even on the resulting (42) 45 [48] sts.

When piece measures (12¹/₄"/31cm) 14¹/₄"/36cm [16¹/₄"/41cm], dec 1 st every 8th row 3 times at armhole edge.

When piece measures (15"/38cm) 17"/43cm [19³/₄"/50cm], beg shaping armhole: BO 5 sts at armhole edge once.

When piece measures (18³/₄"/47.5cm) 21"/53.5cm [24¹/₄"/61.5cm], beg shaping neck: On alt rows, beg at neck edge, BO (7 sts twice) 8 sts once, then 7 sts once [9 sts once, then 8 sts once].

When piece measures (19¹/₄"/49cm) 21¹/₂"/55cm [24³/₄"/63cm], BO the rem (20) 22 [23] sts.

• Right back
Work as for left back, reversing shapings and beg Jacquard Stockinette St at a.

• Sleeves

Using #3/3mm needles and A, CO (47) 49 [53] sts and work
³/₈"/1cm in Single Rib, then cont in Jacquard Stockinette St,
making sure point M on the chart is in the center of the work,
and inc 1 st at each end of every 4th row (11) 13 [14] times.

When piece measures (6 1/4"/16cm) 7"/18cm [8 1/4"/21cm],
BO the resulting (69) 75 [81] sts.

Finishing

Sew the shoulders, sides, and leg seams.

Using #3/3mm needles and A, pick up and K (69) 77 [85] sts
evenly around the neck and work ³/₈"/1cm in Single Rib, then
BO in rib.

Fit and sew in the sleeves.

Sew the zipper into the back and close up the lower back seam.

Striped romper ★★

Sizes
(3 months) 6 months [12 months]

Materials
Any lamb's wool-and-acrylic-blend fingering weight yarn, such as
Phildar's *Lambswool* (51% lamb's wool/49% acrylic; 1³/₄oz/50g =
147yd/134m) in colors: C (lime green–*Perruche/093*),

D (orange–*Curry/076*), F (fuchsia pink–*Fuchsia/004*),
H (peach–*Melon/008*), I (candy pink–*Papaye/015*),
J (burgundy–*Velours/070*), K (pistachio–*Pistache/075*),
L (bronze green–*Bronze/082*), and M (magenta–*Pensée/090*)
For all sizes: 1 ball of each of the colors
1 (12"/30cm) 12"/30cm [14"/35cm] lime green zipper
1 pair #3/3mm knitting needles, or size needed to obtain gauge
1 spare needle or stitch holder

Stitches
Single Rib: See llama romper instructions.
Stockinette Stitch: See llama romper instructions.
Striped Stockinette Stitch: Knit 6 rows of each color,
alternating L, C, K, D, H, I, F, J, and M.

Gauge
26 stitches and 35 rows to a 4"/10cm square knit in Stockinette
Stitch on #3/3mm needles.

Take the time to make a gauge swatch, which is especially
important if you are substituting the suggested yarn.
If necessary, change needle sizes to obtain the correct gauge.

Making the striped romper

• Front
Begin with right leg.

Using #3/3mm needles and L, CO (26) 29 [32] sts and work
2 rows in Single Rib, then cont even in Striped Stockinette St,
beg with 4 rows in L, and inc 1 st at each end of (every 6th row
4 times, then every 8th row 3 times) every 8th row 7 times
[every 10th row 7 times].

When piece measures (6"/15cm) 7"/18cm [8¼"/21cm], put the
resulting (40) 43 [46] sts on a spare needle or stitch holder.

Work the left leg as the right, then CO 2 sts and pick up the sts
from the right leg. Cont even on the resulting (82) 88 [94] sts.

When piece measures (11½"/29cm) 13½"/34cm [15½"/39cm],
BO 1 st at each end of every 6th row 5 times.

When piece measures (14½"/37cm) 16½"/42cm [18½"/47cm],
beg shaping armholes: BO 4 sts at beg of next 2 rows.

When piece measures (17³/₄"/45cm) 20"/51cm [22½"/57cm],
beg shaping neck: BO (12) 14 [14] sts in the center of the next
row, and complete each side separately. On alt rows, beg at neck
edge, dec (4) 4 [5] sts once, 2 sts once, and 1 st (1) 1 [2] times.

When piece measures (19¼"/49cm) 21½"/55cm [24"/61cm],
BO the rem (19) 21 [22] sts for the shoulder.

• Left back
Using #3/3mm needles and L, CO (26) 29 [32] sts and work
2 rows in Single Rib, then cont in Striped Stockinette St, beg
with 4 rows in L, and inc 1 st at each end of (every 6th row
4 times, then every 8th row 3 times) every 8th row 7 times
[every 10th row 7 times].

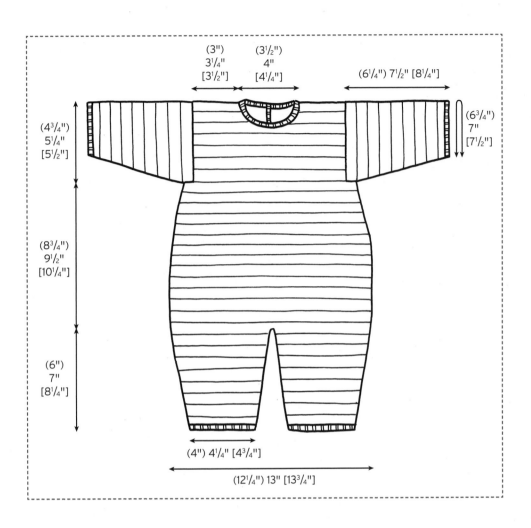

When piece measures (6"/15cm) 7"/18cm [8¼"/21cm] inc 1 st on RH side. Cont even on the resulting (41) 44 [47] sts.

When piece measures (11½"/29cm) 13½"/34cm [15½"/39cm], BO on LH side, 1 st every 6th row 5 times.

When piece measures (14½"/37cm) 16½"/42cm [18½"/47cm], beg shaping armhole: BO 4 sts once at armhole edge.

When piece measures (19"/48cm) 21¼"/54cm [23¾"/60cm], beg shaping neck: On alt rows, beg at neck edge, BO (7 sts once and 6 sts once) 7 sts twice [8 sts twice].

When piece measures (49cm) 55cm [24"/61cm], BO the rem (19) 21 [22] sts for the shoulder.

• Right back
Work as for left back, reversing shapings.

• Sleeves
Using #3/3mm needles and L, CO (45) 47 [49] sts and work 2 rows in Single Rib, then cont in Striped Stockinette St, beg with 4 rows in L and inc 1 st at each end of (every 4th row 4 times, then every 6th row 5 times) every 6th row 10 times [every 4th row 4 times, then every 6th row 8 times].

When piece measures (6¼"/16cm) 7½"/19cm [8¼"/21cm], BO the resulting (63) 67 [73] sts.

Finishing
Sew the shoulders, sides, and leg seams.

Pick up and K (65) 73 [79] sts evenly around the neck in C and work ⅜"/1cm in Single Rib, then BO in rib.

Fit and sew in sleeves. Stitch the zipper into the back opening.

cool kitty

Simple overalls and a cute kitty snuggling sweetly under a soft blanket in juicy citrus colors.

Overalls ★

Sizes
(3 months) 6 months [12 months]

Materials
Any wool-and-acrylic-blend heavy worsted yarn, such as Phildar's *Sport Laine* (51% wool/49% acrylic; 1¾oz/50g = 84yd/76m) in fuchsia pink (*Fuchsia/098*)
3 months: 4 balls
6 months: 4 balls
12 months: 5 balls
2 small pink buttons
1 pair #8/5mm knitting needles, or size needed to obtain gauge
1 spare needle or stitch holder

Stitches
Garter Stitch: K every row.
Left-slanting decrease (SKP): Sl 1 knitwise, K1, PSSO.

Gauge
17 stitches and 34 rows to a 4"/10cm square knit in Garter St on #8/5mm needles.
   Take the time to make a gauge swatch, which is especially important if you are substituting the suggested yarn.
If necessary, change needle sizes to obtain the correct gauge.

Making the overalls

• Back
Begin with a leg.
   Using #8/5mm needles, CO (22) 24 [26] sts and work even in Garter St.
   When piece measures (6¼"/16cm) 7½"/19cm [8¾"/22cm], put the sts on a spare needle or stitch holder.
   Work the 2nd leg to match, then CO 3 sts for the crotch and pick up the sts from the 1st leg. Cont on the resulting (47) 51 [55] sts.
   When piece measures (10¾"/27cm) 12¼"/31cm [13¾"/35cm], beg 1 st from the edge, dec 1 st at each end of every 4th row 5 times (use SKP to dec on RH side and K2tog to dec on LH side).
   When piece measures (13¾"/35cm) 15½"/39cm [17¾"/45cm], beg shaping armholes: On alt rows, beg at armhole edge, BO 3 sts once, 2 sts once, and 1 st once.
   When piece measures (16¼"/41cm) 18¼"/46cm [20½"/52cm], beg shaping neck: BO (7) 7 [9] sts in the center of next row

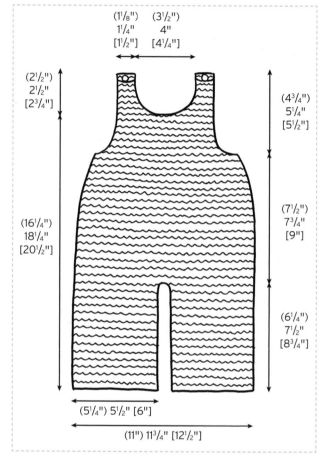

and complete each side separately. On alt rows, beg at neck edge, dec (2) 3 [3] sts once and 1 st twice. Cont even on rem (5) 6 [7] sts. When piece measures (19"/48cm) 20¾"/53cm [23¾"/60cm], BO. Complete other side of neck to match, reversing shapings.

• Front
Work as for back, making a single-st buttonhole in the center of each shoulder strap when the piece measures (18½"/47cm) 20½"/52cm [23¼"/59cm].

Finishing
Sew the side and leg seams.
   Sew the buttons onto the back shoulder straps 3/8"/1cm from the edges.

Patchwork blanket ★

Size
24" x 27"/60 x 68cm

Materials
Any chenille yarn, such as Phildar's *Phil'Chenille* (94% polyester/ 6% polyamide; 1¾oz/50g = 66yd/60m) in colors: A (fuchsia pink–*Fuchsia/005*), B (candy pink–*Starlette/009*), C (lime green–*Anisé/002*), D (burnt orange–*Mandarine/006*), and E (acid orange–*Clémentine/004*)
Quantity: 1 ball of each color
1 pair #8/5mm knitting needles, or size needed to obtain gauge

Stitches
Garter Stitch: See overalls instructions.

Gauge
See overalls instructions.

Making the patchwork blanket
Using #8/5mm needles and A, CO 17 sts, then CO 17 sts B, 17 sts C, 17 sts D, and 17 sts E. Knit 36 rows in Garter St, always crossing the yarn over at each color change, then cont foll the chart, knitting 36 rows in each color change.
    After knitting the last row of squares, BO. Weave in the tails.

Cat ★★

Materials
Any chenille yarn, such as Phildar's *Phil'Chenille* (94% polyester/ 6% polyamide; 1¾oz/50g = 66yd/60m) in colors: A (fuchsia pink–*Fuchsia/005*), B (candy pink–*Starlette/009*), C (lime green–*Anisé/002*), D (burnt orange–*Mandarine/006*), and E (acid orange–*Clémentine/004*)
Quantity: 1 ball of each color
Polyester fiber
1 pair #8/5mm knitting needles, or size needed to obtain gauge

Stitches
Stockinette Stitch: K 1 row, P 1 row.
Seed Stitch: *Row 1:* *K1, P1*, rep from * to *. *Row 2:* *P1, K1*. Rep these 2 rows for patt.
Left-slanting decrease (SKP): Sl 1 knitwise, K1, PSSO.
Double decrease (SK2P): Sl 1 knitwise, K2tog, PSSO.

Embroidery
Backstitch: Make a straight stitch and a space. Take the needle back over the space and bring it out the same distance in front of the thread.

A : fuchsia pink   B : candy pink
C : lime green   D : burnt orange   E : acid orange

Duplicate Stitch: Embroider over each Stockinette St, following the line of the original yarn, as shown in the chart.

Gauge
13 stitches and 20 rows to a 4"/10cm square knit in Stockinette St on #8/5mm needles.
    Take the time to make a gauge swatch, which is especially important if you are substituting the suggested yarn.
If necessary, change needle sizes to obtain the correct gauge.

Making the cat

• Back
Using C, CO 17 sts and work in Stockinette St, inc 1 st at each end of every alt row 3 times, then work 6 rows on the resulting 23 sts, and dec 1 st at each end of every 4th row 5 times. Work 12 rows even on the rem 13 sts, then BO.

• Front
Using C, CO 17 sts and work in Stockinette St, inc 1 st at each end of every alt row 4 times, then work 12 rows on the resulting 25 sts and beg to dec. K1, SKP, K8, SK2P, K8, K2tog, K1. Rep these decs every 4th row twice, lining up the decs with those on the previous row. Knit 12 rows even on the rem 13 sts, then BO.

• Front of the head

Begin at the top. Using A, CO 7 sts and work in Stockinette St, inc 1 st at each end of every row 7 times.

Work 6 rows on the resulting 21 sts, then on next row SK2P with the 3 sts in the center. Rep this dec again 2 rows later, then work 4 rows even. BO 2 sts at beg of next 2 rows, 4 sts at beg of foll 2 rows, then BO the rem 5 sts.

• Back of the head

Begin at the top. Using A, CO 7 sts and work in Stockinette St, inc 1 st at each end of every alt row 5 times.

Work 10 rows on the resulting 17 sts, then BO 2 sts at beg of next 2 rows, 4 sts at beg of foll 2 rows, then BO the rem 5 sts.

• Ears

Using D, CO 9 sts and work in Seed St, dec 1 st at each end of every alt row 3 times, then K last 3 sts tog.

• Arms

Using D, CO 17 sts and work even in Stockinette St.

On 5th row: K3, K2tog, K7, K2tog, K3. On 6th row: K2, K3tog, K5, K3tog, K2. On 7th row: K2, K2tog, K3, K2tog, K2. Change to E and cont even on rem 9 sts for 5½"/14cm, then BO.

Work the 2nd arm to match, using colors C and B.

• Legs

Using C, CO 18 sts and work 2 rows of Stockinette St, then cont in D. On the 7th row, beg dec for the upper part of the leg: K8, K2tog, K8. On the foll row: K7, K3tog, K7. Rep K3tog with the 3 sts in the center on each row 3 more times. Then work 5½"/14cm even on the rem 9 sts, and BO.

Work the 2nd leg to match, using colors B and A.

• Tail

Using C, CO 9 sts and work 7½"/19cm in Stockinette St, then dec 1 st at each end of every alt row 3 times. BO the rem 3 sts.

Finishing

Embroider the face of the cat on the front of the head (see chart), beg above the point where dec starts.

Sew the back and front of the head together, leaving an opening at the neck, and sew on the ears.

Assemble the back and front of the body, leaving openings for the head, arms, and legs, and stuff.

Sew the arms, legs and tail, leaving the tops open, then stuff and sew onto the body.

Stuff the head and sew onto the body.

Accessories ★

Size
6 months

Materials
Any chenille yarn, such as Phildar's *Phil'Chenille* (94% polyester/ 6% polyamide; 1¾oz/50g = 66yd/60m) in colors: A (fuchsia pink–*Fuchsia/005*), B (candy pink–*Starlette/009*), C (lime green–*Anisé/002*), D (burnt orange–*Mandarine/006*), and E (acid orange–*Clémentine/004*)
Quantity: 1 ball of each color
2 pairs #8/5mm knitting needles, or sizes needed to obtain gauge

Stitches
Garter Stitch: See overalls instructions.
Stockinette Stitch: See cat instructions.
Seed Stitch: See cat instructions.

Embroidery
See cat instructions.

Gauge
See cat instructions.

Making the accessories

• Bootie socks
Begin with the sole.

Using B, CO 5 sts and, working in Jacquard Stockinette St and color E, foll the patt in the chart for the sole. At same time, inc 1 st at each end of 1st patt row and dec 1 st at each end of last patt row. BO the rem 5 sts.

For the foot, using A, CO 31 sts and work 6 rows in Stockinette St, then cut the yarn. Put the 13 sts at either end on the spare needles, and cont working only on the 5 sts in the center to make the upper part of the bootie sock. *K4, sl 1 knitwise, K1, PSSO, incorporating the 1st of the reserve sts, turn, P4, Sl 1 purlwise, P1, PSSO, incorporating one of the reserve sts*. Rep from * to * until only 7 sts rem in reserve at either end. Cut the yarn. Pick up the 7 sts on RH side, the 5 sts on the upper part of the bootie sock, and the 7 sts on LH side. Knit 10 rows on the resulting 19 sts, and BO.

Make a 2nd bootie sock in the same way, using colors C and E for the sole, and D for the foot.

Weave in the tails, then stitch the sole to the upper part of the bootie sock and sew the seams.

• Cat hat
Using C, CO 55 sts and work even in Stockinette St.

When piece measures 2"/5cm, beg dec as foll: K12, K3tog, K25, K3tog, K12. Rep these decs every alt row 6 times, lining up the decs with those on the previous row, then BO the rem 27 sts.

For the ear: Using D, CO 11 sts and work in Seed St, dec 1 st at each end of every alt row 4 times, then knit the last 3 sts tog. Make a 2nd ear to match the 1st ear.

Sew the hat, then embroider the face (see chart), beg ⅝"/1.5cm from the bottom edge. Sew the ears on the top.

• Scarf
Using E, CO 90 sts and, working in Garter St, knit 4 rows E, 4 rows D, 4 rows C, 4 rows B, and 4 rows A. At the same time, make a slit on the 2nd row of C: K16, BO 10 sts, and K64. CO the 10 sts again on the next row. BO, then weave in the tails.

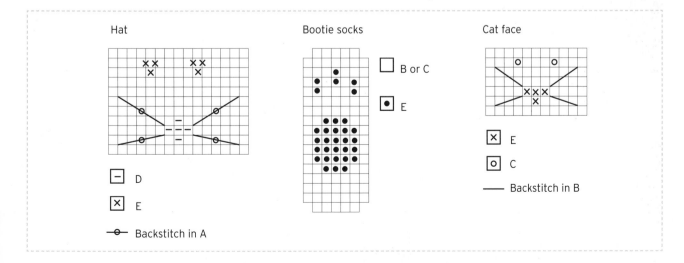

everyone's favorite rib

Simple shapes, a single stitch, and stripes of bright, candy-colored yarn create a dynamic outfit.

Sweater ★★

Sizes
(3 months) 6 months [12 months]

Materials
Any lamb's wool-and-acrylic-blend fingering weight yarn, such as Phildar's *Lambswool* (51% lamb's wool/49% acrylic; 1¾oz/50g = 147yd/134m) in colors: A (charcoal–*Minerai/094*), B (apple green–*Pomme/099*), C (lime green–*Perruche/093*), and D (jade–*Curaçao/002*)
3 months: 2 balls A and a small amount of the other 3 colors
6 months: 3 balls A and a small amount of the other 3 colors
12 months: 4 balls A and a small amount of the other 3 colors
2 4"/10cm black zippers
1 pair #3/3mm knitting needles, or size needed to obtain gauge

Stitches
Double Rib: *K2, P2*, rep from * to *.
Broad-striped Double Rib: *10 rows A, next 2 rows: 1st row, work the knit sts in A and the purl sts in C; 2nd row, work the sts with the same colors; then work 10 rows A, 2 rows A and B, 10 rows A, 2 rows A and D*, rep from * to *.
Left-slanting decrease (SKP): Sl 1 knitwise, K1, PSSO.
Double decrease (SK2P): Sl 1 knitwise, K2tog, PSSO.

Gauge
33 stitches and 37 rows to a 4"/10cm square knit in Double Rib slightly relaxed widthwise on #3/3mm needles.

Take the time to make a gauge swatch, which is especially important if you are substituting the suggested yarn. If necessary, change needle sizes to obtain the correct gauge.

Making the sweater

• **Back**
Using #3/3mm needles and A, CO (84) 90 [96] sts and work in Broad-striped Double Rib, beg with (P1) K2 [P1]**.

When piece measures (4¾"/12cm) 5½"/14cm [6¼"/16cm], beg shaping raglans. BO 4 sts at beg of next 2 rows, then*dec 2 sts once and dec 1 st once at each end of every alt row *, rep from * to * 8 times in total, then, 1 st in from the edge, dec 1 st at each end of every alt row (3) 5 [7] times (use K2tog or K3tog to dec on RH side and SKP or SK2P to dec on LH side).

Work even until piece measures (9"/23cm) 10¼"/26cm [11½"/29cm], BO the rem (22) 24 [26] sts.

• **Front**
Work as for back to **.

When piece measures (4¾"/12cm) 5½"/14cm [6¼"/16cm], beg shaping raglans. BO 4 sts at beg of next 2 rows, then *dec 2 sts once and dec 1 st once at each end of every alt row *, rep from

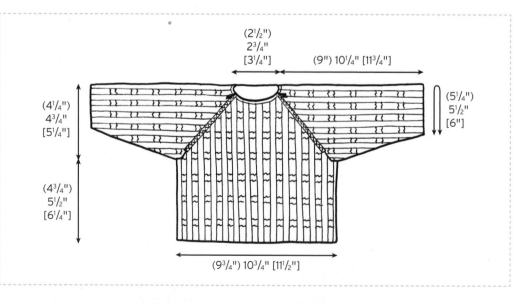

* to * (8) 9 [8] times in total, then 1 st in from the edge, (dec 2 sts once) dec 1 st once [dec 1 st 5 times] at each end of every alt row (use K2tog or K3tog to dec on RH side and SKP or SK2P to dec on LH side).

When piece measures (7¾"/20cm) 9"/23cm [10¼"/26cm], beg shaping neck: BO (6) 8 [12] sts in the center of the next row and complete each side separately. On alt rows, beg at neck edge, BO 2 sts 3 times, 1 st once, and then BO the rem 2 sts.

• **Right sleeve**
Using #3/3mm needles and A, CO (44) 46 [50] sts and work in Broad-striped Double Rib, beg with (P1) K2 [K2], and inc 1 st at each end of (every 2nd row 3 times, then every 4th row 8 times) every 2nd row 3 times, then every 4th row 10 times [every 4th row 14 times].

When piece measures (4¾"/12cm) 5½"/14cm [6¼"/16cm], beg shaping raglans. BO 4 sts at beg of next 2 rows, then work dec on RH side as for the front and on LH side as for the back.

After the last dec on RH side, BO (3 sts once and 2 sts once) 4 sts once and 3 sts once [5 sts twice] every alt row on RH side.

• **Left sleeve**
Make as for right sleeve, reversing shapings.

Finishing
Fit and sew the sleeves to the back raglans.

Using A, pick up and K (34) 38 [46] sts evenly along the top of the sleeves and back neck and K 1 row, binding off as you knit. Knit a similar edging along the front, picking up (38) 42 [46] sts. Sew the zippers into the front raglans. Sew the sleeves and side seams of the sweater.

Pants ★

Sizes
(3 months) 6 months [12 months]

Materials
Any lamb's wool-and-acrylic-blend fingering weight yarn, such as Phildar's *Lambswool* (51% lamb's wool/49% acrylic; 1¾oz/50g = 147yd/134m) in colors: B (apple green–*Pomme/099*), C (lime green–*Perruche/093*), and D (jade–*Curaçao/002*)
For all sizes: 1 ball of each color
1 pair #3/3mm knitting needles, or size needed to obtain gauge
1 spare needle or stitch holder

Stitches
Double Rib: See sweater instructions.
Striped Double Rib: *4 rows C, 4 rows B, 4 rows D*, rep from * to *.

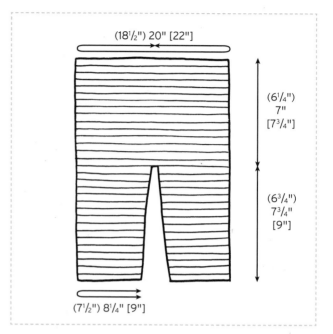

Gauge
33 stitches and 37 rows to a 4"/10cm square knit in Double Rib slightly relaxed widthwise on #3/3mm needles.

Take the time to make a gauge swatch, which is especially important if you are substituting the suggested yarn.
If necessary, change needle sizes to obtain the correct gauge.

Making the pants
The pants are knitted in one piece, beg with the right leg.

Using #3/3mm needles and C, CO (62) 68 [76] sts and work in Striped Double Rib, beg with P1, K2, and inc 1 st at each end of (every 8 rows 3 times, then every 10th row 3 times) every 10th row 3 times, then every 12th row 3 times [every 12th row 3 times, then every 14th row 3 times].

When piece measures (6¾"/17cm) 7¾"/20cm [9"/23cm] (or (64) 74 [86] rows), put the resulting (74) 80 [88] sts on a spare needle or stitch holder.

Work the left leg the same way, beg the rib with (K1, P2) P1, K2 [P1, K2].

Using (B) C [C], CO 3 sts, then work across the sts from the left leg, CO 4 sts in (B) C [C], pick up sts from the right leg and CO 3 sts in (B) C [C]. Cont even on the resulting (158) 170 [186] sts.

When piece measures (13"/33cm) 15"/38cm [17"/43cm], BO in rib.

Finishing
Sew the back of the pants and the leg seams.

Booties ★★

Sizes
3 months (6 months)

Materials
Any lamb's wool-and-acrylic-blend fingering weight yarn, such as Phildar's *Lambswool* (51% lamb's wool/49% acrylic; 1³⁄₄oz/50g = 147yd/ 134m) in colors: A (charcoal–*Minerai/094*), B (apple green–*Pomme/099*), C (lime green–*Perruche/093*), and D (jade–*Curaçao/002*)
Quantity: ³⁄₄oz/20g A and a small amount of the other 3 colors
1 pair #3/3mm knitting needles, or size needed to obtain gauge
2 spare needles

Stitches
Striped Double Rib: See pants instructions.
Double Rib: See sweater instructions.
Left-slanting decrease (SKP): See sweater instructions.

Gauge
See pants instructions.

Making the booties
Begin with the sole. Using D, CO 11 (13) sts and work 28 (32) rows in Striped Double Rib, then BO.

For the foot, using A, CO 62 (68) sts and work in Double Rib, beg with P2 (P1, K2). Work 8 rows, then put 27 (29) sts at either end on a spare needle and cont on the center 8 (10) sts to make the upper part of the bootie. Work *7 (9) sts, then SKP, incorporating the 1st of the reserve sts, turn*, rep from * to * until only 19 (21) sts rem in reserve at either side. Cut the yarn.

Pick up the 19 (21) sts on RH side, the 8 (10) sts from the upper part of the bootie, then the 19 (21) sts on LH side. Work 1¼"/3cm in Double Rib on the 46 (52) sts, then BO in rib.

Sew the back of the bootie and sew on the sole.

Knit a 2nd bootie to match the 1st bootie.

Hat ★

Size
One size

Materials
Any lamb's wool-and-acrylic-blend fingering weight yarn, such as Phildar's *Lambswool* (51% lamb's wool/49% acrylic; 1³⁄₄oz/50g = 147yd/134m) in colors: A (charcoal–*Minerai/094*), B (apple green–*Pomme/099*), C (lime green–*Perruche/093*), and D (jade–*Curaçao/002*)
Quantity: 1 ball A and a small amount of the other 3 colors
1 pair #3/3mm knitting needles, or size needed to obtain gauge

Stitches
Broad-striped Double Rib: See sweater instructions.

Gauge
See sweater instructions.

Making the hat
Using #3/3mm needles and A, CO 54 sts and work 5½"/14cm in Broad-striped Double Rib, then BO.

Work a 2nd piece to match.

Sew the 2 pieces together along 3 sides.

Scarf ★

Materials
Any lamb's wool-and-acrylic-blend fingering weight yarn, such as Phildar's *Lambswool* (51% lamb's wool/49% acrylic; 1³⁄₄oz/50g = 147yd/134m) in colors: B (apple green–*Pomme/099*), C (lime green–*Perruche/093*), and D (jade–*Curaçao/002*)
Quantity: 1 ball of each color
1 pair #3/3mm knitting needles, or size needed to obtain gauge

Stitches
Striped Double Rib: See pants instructions.

Gauge
See pants instructions.

Making the scarf
Using C, CO 30 sts and work 32"/80cm in Striped Double Rib, then BO in rib.

Little pink riding hood

A roomy, cozy little coat that's great worn over any outfit.

Coat ★

Sizes
(3 months) 6 months [12 months]

Materials
Any supersoft polyamide-wool-and-acrylic-blend bulky weight yarn, such as Phildar's *Partner* (50% polyamide/25% combed wool/ 25% acrylic; 1¾oz/50g = 66 m/72yd) in deep pink (*Petunia/016*)
3 months: 5 balls
6 months: 7 balls
12 months: 8 balls
4 pink shank buttons
1 pair #7/4.5mm knitting needles, or size needed to obtain gauge

Stitches
Garter Stitch: K every row.
Single Rib: *K1, P1*, rep from * to *.

Gauge
20 stitches and 38 rows to a 4"/10cm square knit in Garter St on #7/4.5mm needles.

Take the time to make a gauge swatch, which is especially important if you are substituting the suggested yarn.
If necessary, change needle sizes to obtain the correct gauge.

Making the coat

• Back
Using #7/4.5mm needles, CO (60) 64 [68] sts and work in Garter St, dec 1 st at each end of every (14) 18 [22] rows 4 times.

When piece measures (7"/18cm) 8¼"/21cm [9¾"/25cm], beg shaping armholes: On alt rows, beg at armhole edge, dec 3 sts once, 2 sts once, and 1 st once.

Cont even until piece measures (11"/28cm) 12½"/32cm [14½"/ 37cm], then beg shaping shoulders and neck simultaneously. For the neck, BO (10) 12 [14] sts in the center of the next row and complete each side separately, work 2 rows, then BO 4 sts once at neck edge, and for the shoulders, on alt rows at armhole edge, BO (5 sts once and 6 sts once) 6 sts twice [6 sts once and 7 sts once]. BO the rem sts.

• Right front
Using #7/4.5mm needles, CO (34) 36 [38] sts and work in Garter St, dec 1 st on RH side every (14) 18 [22] rows 4 times. When piece measures (3½"/9cm) 4"/10cm [4¼"/11cm], make a single-st buttonhole 3 sts from front edge. Rep this 3 more times after every (1½"/4cm) 2"/5cm [2½"/6cm].

When piece measures (7"/18cm) 8¼"/21cm [9¾"/25cm], beg shaping armholes: On alt rows, beg at armhole edge, dec 3 sts once, 2 sts once, and 1 st once.

Cont even until piece measures (9¾"/25cm) 11½"/29cm [13"/33cm], then beg shaping neck: On alt rows, beg at neck edge, BO (6) 7 [7] sts once, (3) 3 [4] sts once, 2 sts once, and 1 st twice.

When piece measures (11"/28cm) 12½"/32cm [14½"/37cm], beg shaping shoulders. On alt rows, beg at armhole edge, BO (5 sts once and 6 sts once) 6 sts twice [6 sts once and 7 sts once].

• Left front
Make as for right front, omitting buttonholes.

• Sleeves
Using #7/4.5mm needles, CO (30) 32 [34] sts and work in Garter St, inc 1 st at each end of every 10 rows (5) 6 [7] times.

When piece measures (6¼"/16cm) 7"/18cm [8¼"/21cm], BO at each end of every alt row: 3 sts once, (2) 3 [4] sts once, (1) 2 [2] sts once, then BO the rem (28) 28 [30] sts.

• Hood
Using #7/4.5mm needles, CO (76) 80 [84] sts and work even in Garter St.

When piece measures (4"/10cm) 4¼"/11cm [4¼"/11cm], BO 6 sts at beg of next 2 rows, then *5 sts at beg of foll 2 rows, 6 sts at beg of foll 2 rows *, rep from * to * once more, then dec 1 st at each end of every 8th row 4 times.

When piece measures (10¾"/27cm) 11"/28cm [11½"/29cm], BO the rem (12) 16 [20] sts.

Finishing
Sew the shoulders and side seams of the coat.

Sew the hood and stitch it onto the neck, leaving ¾"/2cm free at each side.

Sew and fit the sleeves.

Sew on the buttons.

Accessories ★★

Sizes
(3 months) 6 months [12 months]

Materials
Any chenille bobble polyamide yarn, such as Phildar's *Bowling* (100% polyamide; ⅞oz/25g = 51yd/47m) in pink blend (*Folk/003*)

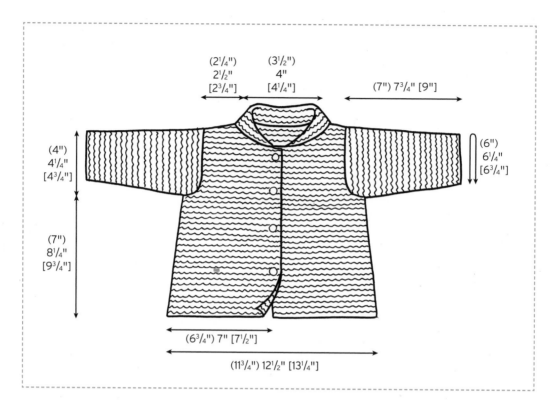

Any lamb's wool-and-acrylic-blend fingering weight yarn, such as Phildar's *Lambswool* (51% lamb's wool/49% acrylic; 1¾oz/50g = 147yd/134m), in fuchsia pink (*Fuchsia/004*)

Quantity: 2 balls A and 1 ball B

1 pair #7/4.5mm knitting needles, or size needed to obtain gauge

Stitches

Single Rib: *K1, P1*, rep from * to *.

To increase: K 1 st in the back of the st in the row below, then K the st above as usual.

Gauge

20 stitches and 28 rows to a 4"/10cm square knit in Single Rib, knitting the 2 yarns together on #7/4.5mm needles.

Take the time to make a gauge swatch, which is especially important if you are substituting the suggested yarn. If necessary, change needle sizes to obtain the correct gauge.

Making the accessories

• Hat

The yarn should be knit double throughout.

Using #7/4.5mm needles, CO (79) 87 [95] sts and work even in Single Rib.

When piece measures (3¼"/8cm) 3½"/9cm [4"/10cm] beg to dec. K8 *K3tog, K (12) 14 [16] sts*, rep from * to * 4 times, then K3tog, K 8 sts. Rep these decs every alt row (3) 4 [5] more times, then every row twice, lining up the decs with those on the previous row. You will be left with (19) 17 [15] sts.

Work 1 row, working the sts 2 at a time, then pass the yarn through the rem (10) 9 [8] sts and pull up to close.

Sew the hat.

• Mittens

The yarn should be knit double throughout.

Using #7/4.5mm needles, CO (21) 23 [25] sts and work in Single Rib. Work 6 rows, then make 4 incs on next row as foll: K1, inc 1, K (9) 10 [11] sts, inc 1, K1, inc 1, K (9) 10 [11] sts, inc 1, K1. Work 2 rows and rep these incs once more. Work 13 rows and beg to dec: K1, K2tog, K (9) 10 [11] sts, K2tog, K1, K2tog, K (9) 10 [11] sts, K2tog, K1. Rep these decs on every alt row (2) 2 [3] more times, lining up the decs with those on the previous row, then BO the rem (17) 19 [17] sts in rib.

Sew the mittens.

Make a braid 27½"/70cm long with the 2 yarns and stitch one end to the inside seam of each mitten.

smart babies

saucy sailor

saucy sailor

Chocolate brown and sky blue—nautical stripes brighten up simple and practical patterns.

Striped cardigan ★

Sizes
(6 months) 12 months [18 months]

Materials
Any wool-and-acrylic-blend sport weight yarn, such as Phildar's *Phil'Laine* (51% wool/49% acrylic, 1¾oz/50g = 138yd/126m) in colors: A (natural–*Lin/098*), B (chocolate brown–*Chocolat/121*), C (denim blue–*Igloo/044*), and D (sky blue–*Ciel/028*)
6 months: 2 balls A and 1 ball each of the other 3 colors
12 months: 3 balls A and 1 ball each of the other 3 colors
18 months: 3 balls A and 1 ball each of the other 3 colors
(5) 6 [6] small wooden 2-hole buttons
1 pair each #3/3mm and #4/3.5mm knitting needles, or sizes needed to obtain gauge

Stitches
Double Rib: *K2, P2*, rep from * to *.
Stockinette Stitch: K 1 row, P 1 row.
Striped Stockinette Stitch: *4 rows B, 4 rows A, 4 rows C, 4 rows D*. Rep from * to *.

Gauge
23 stitches and 30 rows to a 4" (10cm) square knit in Stockinette St on #4/3.5mm needles.

Take the time to make a gauge swatch, which is especially important if you are substituting the suggested yarn.
If necessary, change needle sizes to obtain the correct gauge.

Making the striped cardigan

• Back
Using #3/3mm needles and A, CO (62) 66 [72] sts and work ⅝"/1.5cm in Double Rib, starting with (K2) K2 [P2].

Change to #4/3.5mm needles and work even in Striped Stockinette St until piece measures (7"/18cm) 8"/20cm [9"/22cm], then beg shaping armholes: BO 3 sts at beg of next 2 rows, then 2 sts at beg of next 2 rows and 1 st at beg of next 4 rows.

Cont even until piece measures (12"/30cm) 13"/33cm [14¼"/36cm], then beg shaping neck: BO (14) 16 [18] sts in center of next row, then finish each side separately as foll: work 1 row then BO 6 sts at neck edge of next row. Cont even until piece measures (12¼"/31cm) 13½"/34cm [14½"/37cm] and BO the rem

(11) 12 [14] sts for the shoulder. Work other side to match, reversing shapings.

• Left front
Using #3/3mm needles and A, CO (32) 34 [37] sts and work ⅝"/1.5cm in Double Rib, beg with (P1) K1 [P2]. Change to #4/3.5mm needles and work even in Striped Stockinette St until piece measures (7"/18cm) 7¾"/20cm [8¾"/22cm], then beg shaping armhole: BO 3 sts at beg of next 2 rows, 2 sts at beg of next 2 rows, then 1 st at beg of next 2 rows.

Cont even until piece measures (10¾"/27cm) 11¾"/30cm [13"/33cm], then beg shaping neck: On alt rows, beg at neck edge, BO 6 sts, then (3) 4 [5] sts, then 3 sts, then 1 st twice.

When piece measures (12¼"/31cm) 13½"/34cm [14½"/37cm], BO the rem (11) 12 [14] sts for the shoulder.

• Right front
Work as left front, reversing the shapings.

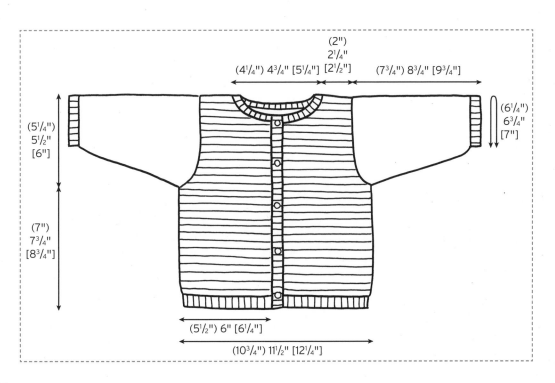

• Sleeves

Using #3/3mm needles and A, CO (36) 40 [42] sts and work
⅝"/1.5cm in Double Rib. Change to #4/3.5mm needles and work
in Stockinette St, inc 1 st at each end of (every 2nd row 3 times,
then every 4th row 9 times) every 4th row 12 times [every 4th
row 14 times].

When piece measures (7"/17.5cm) 7¾"/19.5cm [9"/22.5cm],
BO at beg of each row: 1 st 4 times, 2 sts twice, and 3 sts twice.
BO the rem (46) 50 [56] sts.

Finishing

Sew shoulder seams.

Using #3/3mm needles and B, pick up and K (68) 72 [76] sts
around the neckline and work ⅝"/1.5cm in Double Rib, working
a selvage st at each end of row, then BO in rib.

Using #3/3mm needles and B, pick up and K (68) 76 [84] sts
along the edge of the left front and work 1 row in Double Rib.
On 2nd row, make (5) 6 [6] 2-st buttonholes, the 1st buttonhole
(3) 2 [4] sts from the edge, the rest (13) 12 [13] sts apart. Cont in
rib until band measures ⅝"/1.5cm, then BO in rib.

Work a matching border on the right front, omitting buttonholes.

Set in the sleeves and sew the side and sleeve seams. Sew the
buttons onto the right front in line with the buttonholes.

Overalls ★

Sizes
(6 months) 12 months [18 months]

Materials
Any wool-and-acrylic-blend sport weight yarn, such as
Phildar's *Phil'Laine* (51% wool/49% acrylic, 1¾oz/50g =
138yd/126m) in colors: A (natural–*Lin/098*), B (chocolate
brown–*Chocolat/121*), C (denim blue–*Igloo/044*), and D (sky
blue–*Ciel/028*)

6 months: 3 balls B and 1 ball each of the other 3 colors
12 months: 3 balls B and 1 ball each of the other 3 colors
18 months: 4 balls B and 1 ball each of the other 3 colors
2 small wooden 2-hole buttons
1 pair each #3/3mm needles and #4/3.5mm knitting needles,
or sizes needed to obtain gauge
1 spare needle or stitch holder

Stitches
Double Rib: See striped cardigan instructions.
Stockinette Stitch: See striped cardigan instructions.

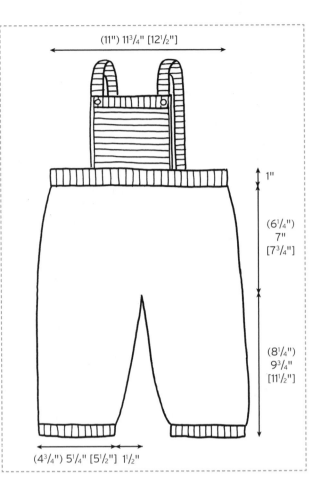

(11") 11¾" [12½"]

1"

(6¼")
7"
[7¾"]

(8¼")
9¾"
[11½"]

(4¾") 5¼" [5½"]   1½"

Striped Stockinette Stitch: *4 rows C, 4 rows D, 4 rows B, 4 rows A*. Rep from * to *.
Left-slanting decrease (SKP): Sl 1 knitwise, K1, PSSO.

Gauge
See striped cardigan instructions.

Making the overalls

• Front
Begin with the right leg.

Using #3/3mm needles and A, CO (28) 30 [32] sts and work ⅝"/1.5cm in Double Rib, starting with (P2) K2 [P2]. Change to #4/3.5mm needles and B and cont in Stockinette St, inc 1 st on the 1st row for size 18 months only. On RH edge of piece, inc 1 st (every 6 rows 9 times) every 6th row 4 times, then every 8 rows 5 times [every 8 rows 7 times, then every 10 rows twice].

When piece measures (8¼"/21cm) 9¾"/25cm [11½"/29cm], put the rem (37) 39 [42] sts on a spare needle or stitch holder.

Work the left leg in the same way, then pick up the sts of the right leg from the spare needle and cont on the resulting (74) 78 [84] sts. On 1st row, K (35) 37 [40], K2tog, SKP, K (35) 37 [40] sts. Rep this on alt rows 4 times, lining up the decs with those on the previous row in the center of piece, then cont on the rem (64) 68 [74] sts.

When piece measures (14½"/37cm) 17"/43cm [19¼"/49cm], change to #3/3mm needles and A and work 1"/2.5cm in Double Rib, then BO in rib.

• Back
Work as for front.

• Bib
Using #4/3.5mm needles and C, CO 32 sts and work 36 rows in Striped Stockinette St, then change to #3/3mm needles and D and work 2 rows in Double Rib. On 3rd row make a single-stitch buttonhole 2 sts from each end of the row and cont in rib until piece measures ⅝"/1.5cm, then BO in rib. Make a selvage st at each end of these rib rows.

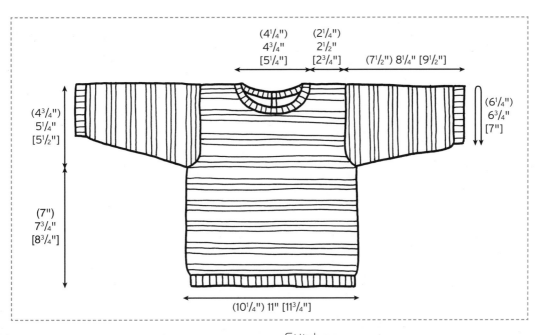

Using #4/3.5mm needles and D, pick up and K 26 sts on either side of the bib, BO as you knit.

• Suspenders

Using #3/3mm needles and D, CO 64 sts and work 1"/2.5cm in Double Rib, then BO in rib. Make a second suspender in the same way.

Finishing

Sew the back to the front.

Sew bib to WS of front at base of rib.

Sew suspenders to back, 3"/8cm apart, then sew a button to end of each suspender.

Striped sweater ★

Sizes

(6 months) 12 months [18 months]

Materials

Any wool-and-acrylic-blend sport weight yarn, such as Phildar's *Phil'Laine* (51% wool/49% acrylic, 1¾oz/50g = 138yd/126m) in colors: A (natural–*Lin/098*), B (chocolate brown–*Chocolat/121*), C (denim blue–*Igloo/044*), and D (sky blue–*Ciel/028*)
6 months: 1 ball of each color
12 months: 2 balls A and 1 ball each of the other 3 colors
18 months: 2 balls A and 1 ball each of the other 3 colors
3 small wooden 2-hole buttons
1 pair each #3/3mm and #4/3.5mm knitting needles, or sizes needed to obtain gauge

Stitches

Double Rib: See striped cardigan instructions.
Stockinette Stitch: See striped cardigan instructions.
Striped Stockinette Stitch: *2 rows D, 2 rows C, 4 rows B, 2 rows C, 2 rows D, 4 rows A*. Rep from * to *.

Gauge

See striped cardigan instructions.

Making the striped sweater

• Back

Using #3/3mm needles and A, CO (60) 64 [70] sts and work ⅝"/1.5cm in Double Rib. Change to #4/3.5mm needles and cont even in Striped Stockinette St until piece measures (7"/18cm) 7¾"/20cm [8¾"/22cm], then beg shaping armholes: BO 2 sts at beg of next 2 rows, then 1 st at beg of next 6 rows.**

When piece measures (7½"/19cm) 8¾"/22cm [9¾"/25cm], beg the back opening. BO the center 2 sts of next row, then cont on LH sts.

When piece measures (11¼"/28.5cm) 12½"/31.5cm [13½"/34.5cm], beg shaping neck: BO 9 sts at neck edge at beg of next row, work 1 row, then BO (3) 4 [5] sts at beg of next row. Work even until piece measures (11¾"/30cm) 13"/33cm [14¼"/36cm], then BO the rem (12) 13 [15] sts.

Work the other side in the same way, reversing shapings.

• Front

Work as for back to **.

When piece measures (10¼"/26cm) 11½"/29cm [12½"/32cm], beg shaping neck: BO center (12) 14 [16] sts of next row and work each side separately. Beg at neck edge, on alt rows, BO 3 sts, 2 sts, then 1 st twice.

When piece measures (12"/30cm) 13"/33cm [14"/36cm], BO the rem (12) 13 [15] sts for shoulder. Work other side to match, reversing shapings.

• Sleeves

Using #3/3mm needles and A, CO (36) 40 [42] sts and work ⅝"/1.5cm in Double Rib. Change to #4/3.5mm needles and work in Striped Stockinette St, inc 1 st at each end of (every 4th row 10 times) every 4th row 7 times, then every 6th row 3 times [every 4th row 5 times, then every 6th row 6 times].

Work even until piece measures (6¾"/17cm) 7½"/19cm [8¾"/22cm], then BO 2 sts at beg of next 2 rows and 1 st at beg of next 4 rows. BO rem (48) 52 [56] sts.

Finishing

Sew the shoulders.

Using #3/3mm needles and A, pick up and K (64) 68 [72] sts around the neck and work ⅝"/1.5cm in Double Rib, making a selvage st at both ends of rows, then BO in rib.

Using #3/3mm needles and A, pick up and K 30 sts on the LH edge of the opening and work 1 row in Double Rib. On the second row, make 3 buttonholes, the 1st buttonhole 6 sts from the edge and the others 8 sts apart. Cont in rib until band measures ⅜"/1cm, then BO in rib.

Make a similar band on the RH side, omitting buttonholes.

Place the 2 border bands together and sew up at base.

Set in the sleeves, sew the sleeve and side seams.

Sew the buttons onto the RH side of the opening in line with the buttonholes.

Blue sweater ★

Sizes

(6 months) 12 months [18 months]

Materials

Any wool-and-acrylic-blend sport weight yarn, such as Phildar's *Phil'Laine* (51% wool/49% acrylic, 1¾oz/50g = 138yd/126m) in D (sky blue–*Ciel/028*)

6 months: 3 balls
12 months: 4 balls
18 months: 4 balls
3 small wooden 2-hole buttons
1 pair each #3/3mm and #4/3.5mm knitting needles, or sizes needed to obtain gauge

Gauge

See striped sweater instructions.

Making the blue sweater

Follow the instructions for the striped sweater but work in plain Stockinette St.

Socks ★★

Sizes

6 months (12 months) 18 months

Materials

Any wool-and-acrylic-blend sport weight yarn, such as Phildar's *Phil'Laine* (51% wool/49% acrylic, 1¾oz/50g = 138yd/126m) in D (sky blue–*Ciel/028*)

6 months: ¾oz/20g
12 months: ⅞oz/25g
18 months: 1oz/30g
1 pair #3/3mm knitting needles, or size needed to obtain gauge

Stitches

Double Rib: See striped cardigan instructions.
Stockinette Stitch: See striped cardigan instructions.
Left-slanting decrease (SKP): See overalls instructions.

Gauge

26 stitches and 32 rows to a 4"/10cm square knit in Stockinette St on #3/3mm needles.

Take the time to make a gauge swatch, which is especially important if you are substituting the suggested yarn.
If necessary, change needle sizes to obtain the correct gauge.

Making the socks

Using #3/3mm needles, CO (34) 38 [42] sts and work ⅝"/1.5cm of Double Rib, then cont in Stockinette St, dec 2 sts evenly spaced in the 1st row.

When piece measures (2¾"/7cm) 3¼"/8cm [3½"/9cm], beg shaping heel: K (9) 10 [12], turn, sl 1, P (8) 9 [11], turn, sl 1, K (7) 8 [10], turn, sl 1, P (7) 8 [10], turn, sl 1, K (6) 7 [9], turn, sl 1, P (6) 7 [9]. Cont in this way until (4) 5 [6] sts rem, then cont as foll: sl 1, K (3) 4 [5], turn, sl 1, P (3) 4 [5], turn, sl 1, K (4) 5 [6], turn, sl 1, P (4) 5 [6], turn, cont until (9) 10 [12] sts rem, then work 1 row across all the sts. Form the other half of the heel in the same way on the (9) 10 [12] sts, beg at the LH edge. Go back to working on all the sts and work even for (1⅜"/3.5cm) 1¾"/4.5cm [2"/5cm], then form toe: K (7) 8 [9], K2tog, SKP, K (12) 14 [16], K2tog, SKP, K (7) 8 [9]. Rep these decs on alt rows (5) 5 [6] times, then, for sizes 12 months and 18 months only, K2tog along the entire next row. Sl the yarn through the rem (8) 6 [6] sts and pull it tight to close the sock.

Work a second sock in the same way.

the perfect ensemble

A matching outfit, drawstring diaper bag, and handy wall organizer:
an ideal trousseau for a style-conscious baby and a well-ordered nursery.

Overalls ★

Sizes
(3 months) 6 months [12 months]

Materials
Any lamb's wool-and-acrylic-blend fingering weight yarn, such
as Phildar's *Lambswool* (51% lamb's wool/49% acrylic; 1¾oz/50g
= 145yd/134m) in dusky purple (*Bruyère/202*)
3 months: 3 balls
6 months: 3 balls
12 months: 4 balls
1 pair each #2/2.5mm and #3/3mm knitting needles, or sizes
needed to obtain gauge
2 small wooden 2-hole buttons
1 spare needle or stitch holder

Stitches
Garter Stitch: K every row.
Pattern: follow the chart.

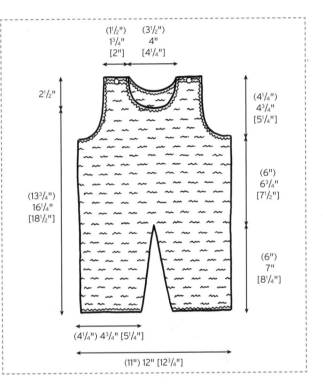

		K1 on right side and P1 on wrong side
	×	P1 on right side and K1 on wrong side

Gauge
26 stitches and 35 rows to a 4"/10cm square knit in pattern on
#3/3mm needles.
 Take the time to make a gauge swatch, which is especially
important if you are substituting the suggested yarn.
If necessary, change needle sizes to obtain the correct gauge.

Making the overalls

• Back
Beg with the left leg.
 Using #2/2.5mm needles, CO (28) 31 [34] sts and work 4 rows
in Garter St.
 Change to #3/3mm needles and cont working, foll the patt,
beg at a on the chart and inc 1 st (every 6 rows 8 times) every
6 rows 8 times [every 8 rows 8 times], on RH edge.
 When piece measures (6"/15cm) 7"/18cm [8¼"/21cm], put the
resulting (36) 39 [42] sts on a spare needle or stitch holder.

 Make the right leg in the same way, reversing shapings and
starting the patt at (b) a [c] on the chart, then CO 1 st for the
crotch and work across the sts of left leg from the spare
needle. Cont working on resulting (73) 79 [85] sts until piece
measures (13¾"/35cm) 15½"/39cm [17¾"/45cm], then beg
shaping armholes: BO (4) 5 [5] sts at beg of next 2 rows, 2 sts
at beg of next 4 rows, then 1 st at each end of every 4 rows
3 times.**
 When piece measures (15"/38cm) 17"/43cm [19"/48cm], beg
shaping neck: CO the (9) 11 [13] center sts of next row and finish
each side separately. Beg at neck edge on alt rows, BO 3 sts
once, 2 sts once, then 1 st (2) 2 [3] times.
 When piece measures (17¼"/44cm) 19¾42"/50cm [22"/56cm],
change to #2/2.5mm needles and work 3 rows in Garter St on
the rem (11) 12 [13] sts, then BO. Work other side to match.

• Front
Work as for back to **.
 When piece measures (13¾"/35cm) 15¾"/40cm [17¾"/45cm],
beg shaping neck: On next row, BO the (9) 11 [13] center sts and
finish each side separately. Beg at neck edge on alt rows, BO
3 sts once, 2 sts once, then 1 st (2) 2 [3] times.

When piece measures (15¾"/40cm) 18¼"/46cm [20½"/52cm], make a single-st buttonhole in the center of the suspender.

When piece measures (16¼"/41cm) 18½"/47cm [20¾"/53cm], change to #2/2.5mm needles and work 3 rows in Garter St on the rem (11) 12 [13] sts, then BO. Work other side to match.

Finishing

Using #2/2.5mm needles, pick up and K (49) 59 [69] sts around neck of back and work 3 rows in Garter St, then BO.

Work the same border on the front neck.

Sew the leg seams.

Using #2/2.5mm needles pick up and K (72) 78 [84] sts around armholes and work 3 rows in Garter St, then BO.

Sew the buttons onto the back suspenders, ⅜"/1cm from end.

Jacket ★

Sizes

(6 months) 12 months [18 months]

Materials

Any lamb's wool-and-acrylic-blend fingering weight yarn, such as Phildar's *Lambswool* (51% lamb's wool/49% acrylic; 1¾oz/50g = 145yd/134m) in teal (*Paon/203*)

6 months: 4 balls
12 months: 4 balls
18 months: 4 balls

1 pair each #2/2.5mm and #3/3mm knitting needles, or sizes needed to obtain gauge

(3) 3 [4] small wooden 2-hole buttons

(39"/1m) 43"/1.10m [47"/1.20m] cream-colored rickrack braid

Stitches

Garter Stitch: See overalls instructions.
Stockinette Stitch: K 1 row, P 1 row.
Left-slanting decrease (SKP): Sl 1 knitwise, K1, PSSO.

Gauge

26 stitches and 52 rows to a 4"/10cm square knit in Garter St on #3/3mm needles.

Take the time to make a gauge swatch, which is especially important if you are substituting the suggested yarn.

If necessary, change needle sizes to obtain the correct gauge.

Making the jacket

• Back

Using #3/3mm needles, CO (75) 81 [85] sts and work 4 rows in Garter St and ⅜"/1cm in Stockinette St, then work even in Garter St until piece measures (5¼"/13cm) 6"/15cm [6¾"/17cm]. Beg shaping armhole: 1 st in from the ends of alt rows, dec 1 st 6 times (use K2tog to dec at RH edge and SKP to dec at LH edge).

When piece measures (9½"/24cm) 10¾"/27cm [11¾"/30cm], beg shaping neck: BO the (15) 17 [19] center sts of next row and finish each side separately: BO 6 sts at neck edge, then work even until piece measures (9¾"/25cm) 11"/28cm [12¼"/31cm], and BO the rem (18) 20 [21] sts.

• Right front

Using #3/3mm needles, CO (39) 42 [44] sts and work 4 rows in Garter St and ⅜"/1cm in Stockinette St, then work even in Garter St until piece measures (5¼"/13cm) 6"/15cm [6¾"/17cm], then beg shaping neck and armhole: 1 st in from RH edge, dec 1 st

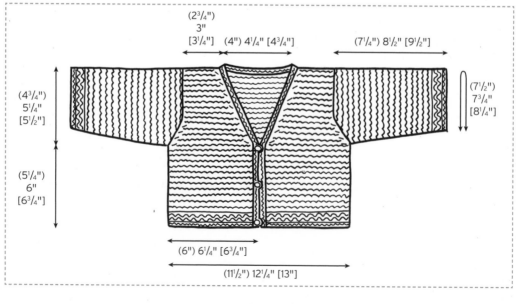

(K2tog) every 4 rows (15) 16 [17] times, and 1 st in from LH edge, dec 1 st (SKP) 6 times every other row.

When piece measures (9¾"/25cm) 11"/28cm [12¼"/31cm], BO the rem (18) 20 [21] sts.

• Left front

Work as for right front, reversing shapings.

• Sleeves

Using #3/3mm needles, CO (49) 52 [55] sts and work 4 rows in Garter St and ³⁄₈"/ 1cm in Stockinette St, then cont in Garter St, inc 1 st every 10 rows (7 times) 8 times [9 times] 1 st in from each edge.

When piece measures (6¼"/16cm) 7½"/19cm [8¾"/22cm], 1 st in from each end, dec 1 st on alt rows 6 times, then BO the rem (51) 56 [61] sts.

Finishing

Sew the rickrack braid on the rows of Stockinette St.

Sew shoulder seams.

Using #2/2.5mm needles, pick up and K (70) 78 [86] sts along the right front edge, then (30) 33 [36] sts around the back neck, and (70) 78 [86] sts down the left front edge. Work 4 rows in Garter St, then BO.

Set in the sleeves, and sew sleeve and side seams.

Embroider (3) 3 [4] button loops on the edge of right front, and sew the buttons on the left front in line with the loops.

Multi-pocket organizer ★

Size

17¾"/45cm x 17¾"/45cm

Materials

Any lamb's wool-and-acrylic-blend fingering weight yarn, such as Phildar's *Lambswool* (51% lamb's wool/49% acrylic; 1³⁄₄oz/50g = 145yd/134m) in colors: A (teal–*Paon/203) and* B (dusky purple–*Bruyère/202)*

Quantity: 3 balls A and 2 balls B

1 pair #3/3mm knitting needles, or size needed to obtain gauge
39"/1m cream-colored rickrack braid
17¾"/45cm x 17¾"/45cm piece iron-on interfacing (nonwoven)
4 large and 3 small wooden 2-hole buttons

Stitches

Garter Stitch: See overalls instructions.
Stockinette Stitch: See jacket instructions.

Gauge

26 stitches and 35 rows to a 4"/10cm square knit in Stockinette St on #3/3mm needles.

Take the time to make a gauge swatch, which is especially important if you are substituting the suggested yarn. If necessary, change needle sizes to obtain the correct gauge.

Making the organizer

• Back panel

Using #3/3mm needles and A, CO 117 sts and work 2 rows in Garter St, then cont even in Stockinette St. When piece measures 17½"/44.5cm, work 3 rows in Garter St, then BO.

Pick up and K 117 sts along one of the sides and K 1 row, then BO. Rep on other side.

• Large pocket

Using #3/3mm needles and B, CO 117 sts and work even in Stockinette St until piece measures 7"/18cm, then work 3 rows in Garter St and BO.

• Small pocket

Using #3/3mm needles and A, CO 117 sts and work even in Stockinette St until piece measures 4¼"/10.5cm, then work 3 rows in Garter St and BO.

• Hanging straps

Using #3/3mm needles and B, CO 12 sts and work 7¾"/20cm in Garter St, then BO.

Make 3 more straps in the same way.

- **Pocket strap**

Using #3/3mm needles and B, CO 12 sts and work 1¼"/3cm in Garter St, then make a single-st buttonhole in the center.

Work even until piece measures 2"/5cm, then BO.

- **Pocket flap**

Using #3/3mm needles and B, CO 29 sts and work 1¼"/3cm in Stockinette St, then make a 2-st buttonhole 4 sts from the edge.

Work even until measures 1¾"/4.5cm, then work 3 rows in Garter St and BO.

Pick up and K 14 sts on each end of the flap and K 1 row, BO as you knit.

Finishing

Sew on the rickrack braid ⅝"/1.5cm from the top of the large pocket and along the bottom of the small pocket.

Sew the large pocket to the back panel ¾"/2cm from the bottom, close to the Garter St edging at each end, and sew the small pocket 2¾"/7cm above it.

Divide the large pocket into 2 with a line of stitching down the center. Divide the small pocket into 4 with a line of stitching at 6"/15cm from the edge, then 2 more lines spaced at 4¾"/12cm and 3¼"/8cm respectively.

Sew the strap to the back panel above the 6"/15cm pocket and the flap above the 4¾"/12cm pocket.

Iron on the interfacing to WS of the back panel.

Fold the 4 hanging straps in half and attach them to back panel with a large button.

Sew the small buttons onto the strap and flap of the smaller pockets.

Drawstring bag ★

Size

12½"/32cm x 17¾"/45cm

Materials

Any lamb's wool-and-acrylic-blend fingering weight yarn, such as Phildar's *Lambswool* (51% lamb's wool/49% acrylic; 1¾oz/50g = 145yd/134m) in colors: A (teal–*Paon/203*) and B (dusky purple–*Bruyère/202*)
Quantity: 5 balls B and 1 ball A
98"/210cm cream-colored rickrack braid
1 pair #3/3mm knitting needles, or size needed to obtain gauge
1 #D/3/3mm crochet hook

Stitches

Single Rib: *K1, P1*, rep from * to *.
Stockinette Stitch: See jacket instructions.

Row of holes: *Row 1:* *K3, yo, K2tog*. Rep from * to *.
Row 2: Purl.

Crochet Stitches
Chain Stitch: yo, draw yarn through loop on hook.
Slip Stitch (SL ST): Insert hook in st, yo and draw yarn through both loops.
Single Crochet: Insert hook in st, yo and draw yarn through st, yo and draw yarn through both loops.

Gauge

26 stitches and 35 rows to a 4"/10cm square knit in Stockinette St on #3/3mm needles.

Take the time to make a gauge swatch, which is especially important if you are substituting the suggested yarn.
If necessary, change needle sizes to obtain the correct gauge.

Making the drawstring bag

- **Base**

Using #3/3mm needles and B, CO 25 sts and work in Stockinette St, CO 5 sts at beg of 2nd and 3rd rows, 4 sts at beg of next 2 rows, 3 sts at beg of next 2 rows, 2 sts at beg of next 6 rows, then 1 st at each end of alt rows 9 times and 1 st at each end of every 4th row 3 times.

Work 30 rows on the resulting 85 sts, then dec 1 st at each end of every 4 rows 3 times, then alt rows 9 times. Then BO 2 sts at beg of next 6 rows, 3 sts at beg of next 2 rows, 4 sts at beg of next 2 rows, 5 sts at beg of next 2 rows, then BO the rem 24 sts.

- **Sides**

Using #3/3mm needles and B, CO 132 sts and work in Stockinette St until piece measures 15¾"40cm. Work a row of holes foll by 2"/5cm in Single Rib, then BO.
Make a second side in same way.

Finishing

Sew the rickrack braid to the sides, 1 strip of braid at 2¾"/7cm from the bottom edge and a 2nd strip ¾"/2cm above it.

Place the 2 sides together, RS facing, and join side seams. Sew the sides to the base.

Make a twisted cord 27½"/70cm long from 12 strands of A, each 112"/280cm long. Thread it through the row of holes at the top of the bag. Tie a knot about 1½"/4cm from each end of the cord.

Crochet 2 balls for the ends of the cords: Crochet a 12-st chain in B, close the circle with a SL ST, then crochet 4 rounds in SL ST. Cut the yarn and thread the balls over the knots in the cord, then run a thread around top and bottom of the balls and pull them tight.

warm and chic

warm and chic

Small flowers or hearts worked in Jacquard, for girls or boys: two attractive, chic outfits with stylish details.

Overalls ★★

Sizes
(3 months) 6 months [12 months]

Materials
Any all-wool fingering weight yarn, such as Bouton d'Or's *Baby Superwash* (100% wool; 1¾oz/50g = 219yd/200m) in colors:
A (taupe–*Taupe/570*) and B (silver gray–*Glacier/231*)
3 months: 3 balls A and a small amount of B
6 months: 3 balls A and a small amount of B
12 months: 4 balls A and a small amount of B
2 heart-shaped pearl buttons
1 set #3/3mm double-pointed needles
1 pair #3/3mm knitting needles, or size needed to obtain gauge
1 spare needle or stitch holder
1 round-tipped embroidery needle

Stitches
Stockinette Stitch: K 1 row, P 1 row.
Left-slanting decrease (SKP): Sl 1 knitwise, K1, PSSO.
Increase: Pick up and K loop between 2 sts.

Embroidery Stitches
Duplicate Stitch: Embroider over each Stockinette St, following the line of the original yarn, as shown in the chart.

Gauge
30 stitches and 40 rows to a 4"/10cm square knit in Stockinette St on #3/3mm needles.

Take the time to make a gauge swatch, which is especially important if you are substituting the suggested yarn.
If necessary, change needle sizes to obtain the correct gauge.

Making the overalls

• Front
Begin with the right leg.
Using #3/3mm needles and A, CO (30) 33 [36] sts and work 3 rows of Stockinette St in A, 2 rows B, 3 rows A. On the next row form the hem by knitting each st tog with the corresponding loop of the cast-on edge. Cont working in A. On RH edge, starting 1 st in from the edge, inc 1 st at beg of (every 6th row) alt 6th and 8th rows [every 8th row] 10 times. On the LH edge inc 1 st at beg of alt rows 10 times for all three sizes.

When piece measures (7"/18cm) 8¼"/21cm [9½"/24cm], put the resulting (50) 53 [56] sts on a spare needle or stitch holder.
Work the left leg in the same way, reversing shaping, then pick up the sts of the right leg from the holder and cont in Stockinette St on the resulting (100) 106 [112] sts.
When piece measures (11"/28cm) 12½"/32cm [15"/38cm], on next K row, K1, K2tog, K to 3rd st from end, SKP, K1. Rep 9 times on K rows only.
When piece measures (13"/33cm) 14½"/37cm [17"/43cm], beg shaping armholes: BO 3 sts at beg of next 4 rows, then, forming a selvage st at both edges, dec 1 st at each end (7) 5 [3] times every 2 rows, then (2) 4 [6] times every 4 rows, then 5 times every 2 rows, for all three sizes. (Use K2tog to dec at beg of rows and SKP to dec at end of rows.)**
When work measures (16½"/42cm) 18½"/47cm [20¼"/54cm], put rem (40) 46 [52] sts on a spare needle or stitch holder.

• Back
Work as for front to **.
When piece measures (13"/33cm) 14½"/37cm [17"/43cm], beg shaping armholes as for front.
Still cont shaping as for front, when piece measures

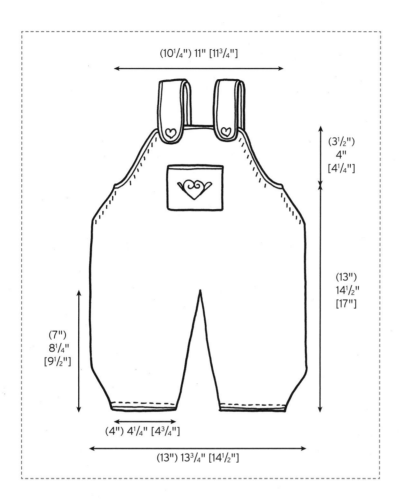

(10¼") 11" [11¾"]

(3½")
4"
[4¼"]

(13")
14½"
[17"]

(7")
8¼"
[9½"]

(4") 4¼" [4¾"]

(13") 13¾" [14½"]

(15½"/39cm) 17¼"/44cm [19¼"/49cm], beg neck opening: BO the 2 center sts of next row, then work each side separately. On alt rows, starting 1 st in from neck edge, dec 1 st (9) 10 [13] times. Cont on the rem (10) 12 [12] sts to form the suspenders. After the last dec for the armhole, work even for (5½"/14cm) 6¼"/16cm [7"/18cm], then form a buttonhole by BO the 2 center sts. Work even for another ⅜"/1cm, then put sts on a spare needle or stitch holder.

• Pocket
Using A, CO 27 sts and work 2½"/6cm of Stockinette St in A, 2 rows B, 2 rows A, then BO.

Finishing
All the borders are worked in the same way.

Using A, pick up and K (31) 34 [37] sts along the left front armhole, K the (40) 46 [52] sts from the holder, dec 8 sts evenly across them, then pick up and K (31) 34 [37] sts along LH armhole. Work 1 row A, 2 rows B, 2 rows A, then BO.

With #3/3mm dpn, pick up and K (77) 87 [97] sts along the RH armhole and suspender of the back, knit the sts from the holder, then pick up and K (50) 57 [64] sts down to the base of the neck opening. Work the border. Work the other side to match.

Sew the side seams of the legs. Fold the borders under, leaving the 2 rows of B showing, and sl st them to WS.

Using B and Duplicate Stitch, embroider the motif (see chart) onto the center of the pocket, fold back and sew the border in the same way, then sew to the center front 2¼"/5.5cm from the top.

Sew the buttons for the suspenders to the front.

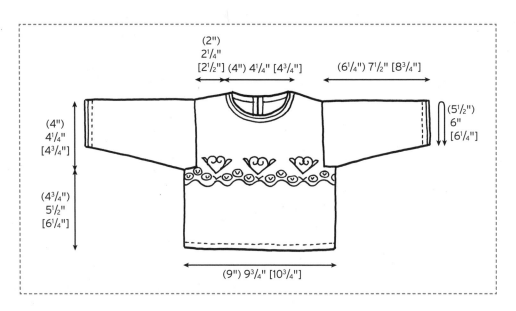

Sweater ★★

Sizes
(3 months) 6 months [12 months]

Materials
Any all-wool fingering weight yarn, such as Bouton d'Or's *Baby Superwash* (100% wool; 1¾oz/50 = 219yd/200m) in colors: A (taupe–*Taupe/570*), B (silver gray–*Glacier/231*), and C (cream–*Naturel/380*)
3 months: 1 ball B, 1 ball A, and a small amount of C
6 months: 1 ball B, 2 balls A, and a small amount of C
12 months: 2 balls B, 2 balls A, and a small amount of C
1 snap fastener
1 set double-pointed #3/3mm needles
1 pair #3/3mm knitting needles, or size needed to obtain gauge

Stitches
Stockinette Stitch: See overalls instructions.
Jacquard Stockinette Stitch: Follow the chart, twisting yarns together at each color change.

Gauge
See overalls instructions.

Making the sweater

• Front
Using #3/3mm needles and B, CO (69) 75 [81] sts and work 8 rows in Stockinette St, then on the next row form a hem by knitting each st tog with the corresponding loop of the cast-on edge. Cont even in Stockinette St until piece measures (3½"/9cm) 4¼"/11cm [5¼"/13cm], then work the 20 rows of Jacquard Stockinette pattern, beg at (a) b [c] on the chart, and cont in Stockinette St using A. At the same time, when piece measures (4¾"/12cm) 5½"/14cm [6¼"/16cm], BO 5 sts at beg of next 2 rows for armholes.

When piece measures (7"/18cm) 8¼"/21cm [9½"/24cm], beg shaping neck: On next row, BO the (9) 13 [15] center sts, then finish each side separately. Beg at neck edge of alt rows, BO 3 sts twice, 2 sts once, and 1 st twice.

When piece measures (8¾"/22cm) 9¾"/25cm [11"/28cm], beg shaping shoulder: BO at beg of alt rows, (5 sts 3 times) 5 sts twice, then 6 sts once [6 sts 3 times]. Work other side of neck to match.

• Back
Using B, CO (69) 75 [81] sts and work in Stockinette St, forming the hem as for front.

When piece measures (4¾"/12cm) 5½"/14cm [6¼"/16cm], BO 5 sts at beg of next 2 rows for the armholes.

When piece measures (6¼"/16cm) 7½"/19cm [8¾"/22cm], beg back opening: CO the center st of next row and finish each side separately.

When piece measures (8½"/21.5cm) 9½"/24.5cm [11"/27.5cm], beg at neck edge, BO 9 sts at beg of next row, then BO (5) 7 [8] sts on next alt row. Cont even until piece measures (8¾"/22cm) 9¾"/25cm [11¼"/28cm], then beg forming shoulder: Starting at armhole edge, BO at beg of alt rows (5 sts 3 times) 5 sts twice, then 6 sts once [6 sts 3 times]. Work other side of neck to match.

• Sleeves
Using A, CO (42) 46 [48] sts and work 3 rows in Stockinette St in A, 2 rows B, and 3 rows A, then form the hem in the same way as for back. Cont in A, inc 1 st at both ends of (every 6 rows

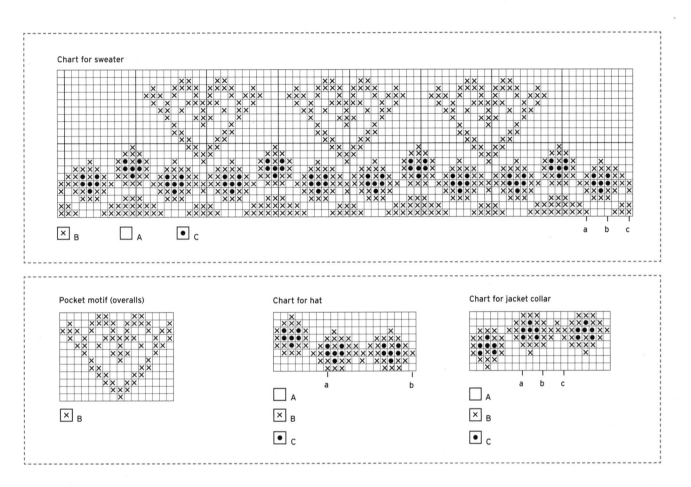

Chart for sweater

☒ B   ☐ A   ⊡ C

Pocket motif (overalls)

☒ B

Chart for hat

a   b

☐ A

☒ B

⊡ C

Chart for jacket collar

a   b   c

☐ A

☒ B

⊡ C

9 times) every 6 rows 7 times, then every 8 rows 3 times [every 6 rows 9 times, then every 8 rows 3 times].

When piece measures (6¼"/16cm) 7½"/19cm [8¾"/22cm, BO the resulting (60) 66 [72] sts.

Finishing

Sew shoulder seams.

Using B, pick up and K 17 sts on each side of the opening and work 6 rows in Stockinette St, then BO. Fold back these borders to form a hem and sl st them to WS of the sweater, then sew the two bottom ends together.

Using #3/3mm dpn and A, finish the neckline by picking up and K (14) 16 [17] sts around LH side of back, (41) 44 [47] sts around front, and (14) 16 [17] sts around RH side of back. Work 2 rows of Stockinette St in A, 2 rows B, and 3 rows A, then BO.

Set in the sleeves, and sew the sleeve and side seams of sweater.

Fold back the neck border, leaving the 2 rows of B showing, and sl st it to WS. Sew the snap fastener to back opening.

Jacket ★★★

Sizes
(3 months) 6 months [12 months]

Materials
Any all-wool fingering weight yarn, such as Bouton d'Or's *Baby Superwash* (100% wool; 1¾oz/50g = 219yd/200m) in colors: A (taupe−*Taupe/570*), B (silver gray−*Glacier/231*), C (cream−*Naturel/380*), and D (pale pink−*Rosée/513*)

3 months: 2 balls Glacier and a small amount of the other 3 colors
6 months: 3 balls Glacier and a small amount of the other 3 colors
12 months: 3 balls Glacier and a small amount of the other 3 colors
(4) 4 [5] heart-shaped pearl buttons
1 pair #3/3mm knitting needles, or size needed to obtain gauge
1 spare needle or stitch holder

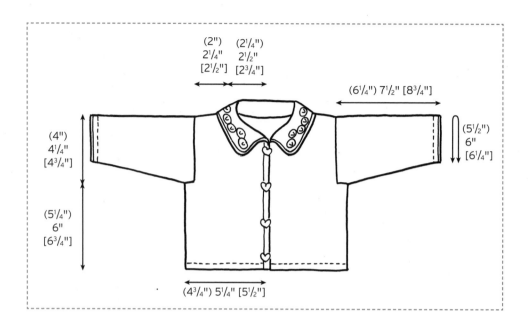

Stitches

Stockinette Stitch: See overalls instructions.
Jacquard Stockinette Stitch: Follow the chart, twisting yarns together at each color change.

Gauge

See overalls instructions.

Making the jacket

• Back

Using #3/3mm needles and B, CO (69) 75 [81] sts and work 8 rows in Stockinette St. On the next row form the hem by knitting each st tog with the corresponding loop of the cast-on edge. Cont working even until piece measures (5¼"/13cm) 6"/15cm [6¾"/17cm], then BO 5 sts at beg of next 2 rows for armholes.

When piece measures (9"/23cm) 10¼"/26cm [11½"/29cm, beg shaping shoulders: BO (5 sts at beg of next 6 rows), 5 sts at beg of next 4 rows, then 6 sts at beg of foll 2 rows [6 sts at beg of next 6 rows], then BO rem (29) 33 [35] sts for the neck.

• Left front

Using #3/3mm needles and B, CO (36) 39 [42] sts and work in Stockinette St, forming a hem in same way as for back.

When piece measures (5¼"/13cm) 6"/15cm [6¾"/17cm], BO 5 sts at RH edge for armhole, then work even until piece measures (7½"/19cm) 8¾"/22cm [9¾"/25cm] and beg shaping neck: BO at neck edge of alt rows, (5) 6 [6] sts, (4) 4 [5] sts, 3 sts, (2) 3 [3] sts, then 1 st twice.

When piece measures (9"/23cm) 10¼"/26cm [11½"/29cm], BO at armhole edge of alt rows (5 sts 3 times) 5 sts twice, then 6 sts once [6 sts 3 times] for shoulder.

• Right front

Work as for left front, reversing the shapings.

• Sleeves

Using #3/3mm needles and B, CO (42) 46 [48] sts and work 3 rows of Stockinette St in B, 2 rows D, 3 rows B, then form the hem as for back and cont in B, inç 1 st at each end of (every 6 rows 9 times) every 6 rows 7 times, then every 8 rows 3 times [every 6 rows 9 times, then every 8 rows 3 times].

When piece measures (6¼"/16cm) 7½"/19cm [8¾"/22cm], BO the resulting (60) 66 [72] sts.

Finishing

Sew the shoulder and side seams of the jacket. Pick up and K (71) 77 [83] sts around the neck in B and work 7 more rows in Stockinette St, then 8 rows in the Jacquard Stockinette St patt, beg at (a) b [c] on the chart, then work 2 more rows in B. Put the sts on a spare needle or stitch holder.

Still working in B, pick up and K 11 sts along the edge of the collar and 2 more on the corner, knit across the (71) 77 [83] sts from the holder, pick up and K 2 sts on corner of collar and 11 along the 2nd edge. Purl the next row in B, then work 2 rows of Stockinette St in D, 2 rows B, then BO.

Pick up and K (57) 66 [74] sts in B along the left front edge, purl next row, then work 2 rows of Stockinette St in B, 2 rows D, 3 rows B, then BO.

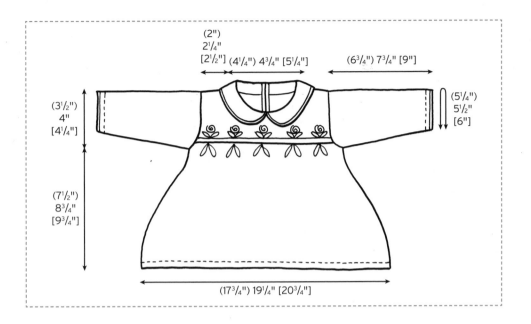

Work a similar border on right front, forming (4) 4 [5] 2-st buttonholes on the 2nd and 5th rows, the 1st buttonhole 2 sts from the edge and the rest (15) 18 [15] sts apart.

Set in the sleeves and sew the seams.

Fold back all the borders, leaving the 2 rows of D showing, and sl st them to WS of the jacket.

Sew the buttons onto the left front in line with the buttonholes.

Hat ★★★

Sizes
(3 months) 6 months [12 months]

Materials
Any all-wool fingering weight yarn, such as Bouton d'Or's *Baby Superwash* (100% wool; 1¾oz/50 = 219yd/200m) in colors: A (taupe–*Taupe/570*), B (silver gray–*Glacier/231*), and C (cream–*Naturel/380*)
For all sizes: 1 ball A and a small amount of B and C
1 pair #3/3mm knitting needles, or size needed to obtain gauge

Stitches
Stockinette Stitch: See overalls instructions.
Jacquard Stockinette Stitch: Follow the chart, twisting yarns together at each color change.

Gauge
See overalls instructions.

Making the hat
Using #3/3mm needles and A, CO (110) 122 [134] sts and work in Stockinette St: 3 rows A, 2 rows B, 3 rows A.

On the next row form a hem by knitting each st tog with the corresponding loop of the cast-on edge. Work 3 rows A, 8 rows in Jacquard Stockinette St patt, beg at (a) b [b] on the chart, 3 rows A, 1 row B, 8 rows A, then on next row form the turn-up band in the same way as a hem, knitting each st tog with corresponding loop from 2nd row of A. Purl 1 row, then on next row dec as foll: 1 selvage st, *K (7) 8 [9], K2tog*, rep from * to * 12 times in all, 1 selvage st. Rep these dec twice more on every 4th row, then (4) 5 [6] times every 2nd row. On next K row, work rem 26 sts as foll: K 1 selvage st, K2tog 12 times, 1 selvage st. On next row: 1 selvage st, P2tog 6 times, 1 selvage st. Work 4 rows on rem 8 sts, then cut the yarn, pass it through the sts, and draw it tight.

Sew the seam.

Dress ★★★

Sizes
(3 months) 6 months [12 months]

Materials
Any all-wool fingering weight yarn, such as Bouton d'Or's *Baby Superwash* (100% wool; 1¾oz/50 = 219yd/200m) in colors: A (taupe–*Taupe/570*), B (silver gray–*Glacier/231*), and D (pale pink–*Rosée/513*)
3 months: 3 balls B and a small amount of the other 2 colors
6 months: 4 balls B and a small amount of the other 2 colors
12 months: 4 balls B and a small amount of the other 2 colors

2 snap fasteners
1 round-pointed embroidery needle
1 cable needle
1 pair #3/3mm knitting needles, or size needed to obtain gauge
1 spare needle or stitch holder

Stitches

Stockinette Stitch: See overalls instructions.

Embroidery Stitch

Bullion Knot: bring needle up and pull yarn to RS, push needle back through work a short distance away, leaving a slack loop, then bring needle partway out again at original exit point. Twist thread of loop 6 or 7 times around needle, then pull it through, keeping coils tight between thumb and forefinger. Push needle back again through 2nd point and pull knot tight. Finish with a retaining st on WS.

Gauge

See overalls instructions.

Making the dress

• Front

Using #3/3mm needles and B, CO (134) 146 [158] sts and work 8 rows in Stockinette St. On the next row form the hem by knitting each st tog with the corresponding loop of the cast-on edge. Work even until piece measures (7½"/19cm) 8¾"/22cm [9¾"/25cm], then beg shaping armholes: BO 3 sts at beg of next 2 rows, 2 st at beg of next 2 rows, and 1 st at beg of next 2 rows.

When piece measures (7¾"/20cm) 9"/23cm [10½"/26cm], dec (60) 66 [72] sts on the next row as foll: K1, then *sl 3 sts onto a cn and place behind the piece, K tog 1 st from LH needle and 1 st from cn 3 times, sl 3 sts onto a cn, place in front of the piece, K tog 1 st from cn and 1 st from LH needle 3 times*. Rep from * to * (10) 11 [12] times in all, then K1. Work 9 more rows in Stockinette St, then on 10th row, form the pleat by knitting each st from LH needle tog with the corresponding loop from the 9th previous row.**

Cont working even in Stockinette St until piece measures (9½"/24cm) 11"/28cm [12½"/32cm], then beg shaping neck: BO the (10) 14 [16] center sts of next row and finish each side separately. Beg at neck edge of alt rows, BO 3 sts twice, 2 sts once, then 1 st 3 times.

When work measures (11"/28cm) 12½"/32cm [14¼"/36cm], beg shaping shoulder: At armhole edge of alt rows, BO (5 sts 3 times) 5 sts twice, then 6 sts once [6 sts 3 times].

• Back

Work as front to **.

Cont working even in Stockinette St until piece measures (8¾"/22cm) 10¼"/26cm [11¾"/30cm], BO the 2 center sts of next row for the opening and finish each side separately.

When piece measures (11"/28cm) 12½"/32cm [14¼"/36cm], beg shaping both shoulder and neck: At neck edge, BO (11) 12 [12] sts, then (4) 5 [6] sts on next alt row. At armhole edge, BO on alt rows (5 sts 3 times) 5 sts twice, then 6 sts once [6 sts 3 times].

• Sleeves

Using #3/3mm needles and B, CO (38) 42 [46] sts and work 3 rows of Stockinette St in B, 2 rows A, 3 rows B, then form the hem as for the front and cont in B, inc 1 st at each end of (every 4 and every 6 rows alternately 10 times) every 6 rows 11 times [every 6 rows 12 times].

When piece measures (6"/15cm) 7"/18cm [8¼"/21cm], BO 3 sts at beg of next 2 rows, 2 sts at beg of next 2 rows, 1 st at beg of next 2 rows, then BO rem (44) 50 [56] sts.

Finishing

Sew the shoulder and side seams. Using B, pick up and K 17 sts on each side of the opening and cont in Stockinette St, working 1 row B, 2 rows A, 2 rows B, then BO.

For half collar, using B and beg at opening, pick up and K (16) 18 [20] sts around back neck, then (21) 23 [25] sts around to center front. Work 1"/2.5cm in Stockinette St, then dec 1 st at each end of next 2 K rows and put sts on a spare needle or stitch holder. Still using B, pick up and K 10 sts along edge of half collar, work across the sts from the holder, then pick up and K 10 sts along other edge. In Stockinette St, work 1 row B, 2 rows A, 2 rows B, then BO.

Work the other half collar in the same way.

Set in the sleeves and sew the seams.

Fold back the collar borders, leaving the 2 rows of B showing, and sl st to WS. Sew back the borders of the opening, sew bases tog then attach top edges to collar.

Sew the snap fasteners on back opening.

Embroider 5 flowers above the pleat, forming 2 Bullion Knots in D for the leaves and 4 Bullion Knots in A for the petals.

sugared almonds

sugared almonds

Simple pastel stripes in Garter Stitch stand out against a Stockinette Stitch background.

Romper ★★

Sizes

3 months (6 months)

Materials

Any wool-and-cashmere-blend sport weight yarn, such as Phildar's *Laine et Cachemire* (85% combed wool/15% cashmere; ⁷⁄₈oz/25g = 65yd/60m) in colors: A (ecru–*Écru/032*), B (pale pink–*Rosée/109*), C (pistachio–*Pistache/108*), and D (candy pink–*Coquille/103*)

3 months: 6 balls A, and 1 ball each of the other 3 colors
6 months: 6 balls A and 1 ball each of the other 3 colors
5 small 2-hole pearl buttons
1 pair each #4/3.5mm and #6/4mm knitting needles, or sizes needed to obtain gauge
1 spare needle or stitch holder

Stitches

Stockinette Stitch: K 1 row, P 1 row.
Garter Stitch: K every row.
Stripe pattern: *Work 4 rows of Garter St in B, 6 rows of Stockinette St in A, 4 rows of Garter St in C, 6 rows of Stockinette St in A, 4 rows of Garter St in D, and 6 rows of Stockinette St in A*. Rep from * to *.
Left-slanting decrease (SKP): Sl 1 knitwise, K1, PSSO.
Double decrease (SK2P): Sl 1 knitwise, K2tog, PSSO.
Make One (M1): Pick up and K or P loop between last st knitted and next st on LH needle.

Gauge

23 stitches and 35 rows to a 4"/10cm square knit in Stripe patt on #6/4mm needles.

Take the time to make a gauge swatch, which is especially important if you are substituting the suggested yarn.
If necessary, change needle sizes to obtain the correct gauge.

Making the romper

The body of the romper is worked in a single piece, beg with the left leg.

Using #4/3.5mm needles and A, CO 60 (64) sts and work 10 rows in Garter St, then change to #6/4mm needles and work in Stripe patt, beg with 2 rows in Stockinette St, M1 st at each end of every 14 (18) rows 3 times.

When piece measures 7¼"/18.5cm (8"/20.5cm), put the resulting 66 (70) sts on a spare needle or stitch holder.

Work right leg in the same way, then CO 6 sts for the crotch and work across sts of left leg from the holder. Cont in Stripe patt on resulting 138 (146) sts for 10 rows, then beg dec as

foll: K32 (34), SK2P, K68 (72), SK2P, K32 (34). Rep these dec every 4 rows 9 times, lining up the decs with those on the previous row.

When piece measures 15¼"/38.5cm (16½"/41.5cm), beg shaping armholes: K21 (23) sts for the right front, BO 2 sts, K52 (58) sts for the back, BO 2 sts, then cont on rem 21 (23) sts to form left front.

When piece measures 18"/45.5cm (19¼"/49cm), beg shaping neck: BO at neck edge of alt rows 3 (4) sts, 2 sts, then 1 st. When piece measures 19"/48.5cm (20½"/52.5cm), BO the rem 15 (16) sts.

Pick up the 21 (23) sts for the right front and work in the same way, reversing shapings.

Pick up the 52 (58) sts for the back and work even until work measures 18¾"/47.5cm (20"/51.5cm), then beg shaping neck: BO the 12 (16) center sts of next row and finish each side separately, BO another 5 sts at neck edge on next alt row.

When piece measures 19"/48.5cm (20½"/52.5cm), BO the rem 15 (16) sts.

Finish the other side in the same way.

• Sleeves

Using #4/3.5mm needles and A, CO 39 (42) sts and work 10 rows of Garter St, then change to #6/4mm needles and cont in Stripe patt, M1 at each end every 10 rows twice, then every 12 rows twice (every 10 rows 3 times, then every 12 rows twice).

When piece measures 7"/18cm (8"/20cm), BO the resulting 48 (52) sts.

Finishing

Using #4/3.5mm needles and A, pick up and K 58 (63) sts along the edge of the left front and work 10 rows in Garter St, then BO.

Make a similar border on the right front, forming four 2-st buttonholes on the 5th row, the 1st buttonhole 11 (12) sts from the end and the rest 10 (11) sts apart.

Sew the shoulder seams.

Using #4/3.5mm needles and A, pick up and K 52 (57) sts around the neck and work 8 rows in Garter St, making a 2-st buttonhole on the 4th row, 2 sts from the right front edge.

Sew the leg seams and the crotch, placing the buttonhole band over the other band.

Set in the sleeves and sew the seams.

Sew on the buttons in line with the buttonholes.

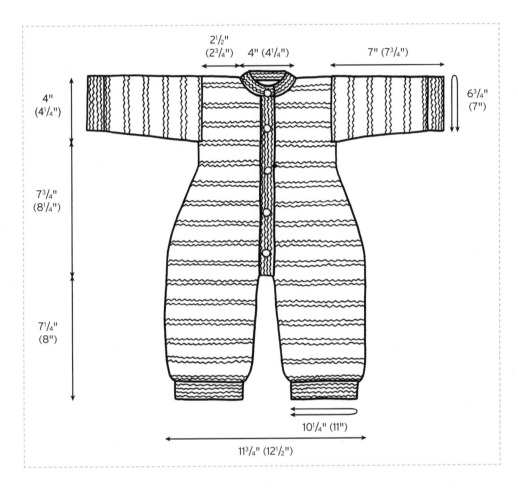

Striped cardigan ★

Sizes

(3 months) 6 months [12 months]

Materials

Any wool-and-cashmere-blend sport weight yarn, such as Phildar's *Laine et Cachemire* (85% combed wool/15% cashmere; ⅞oz/25g = 65yd/60m) in colors: A (ecru–*Écru/032*), B (pale pink–*Rosée/109*), C (pistachio–*Pistache/108*), and D (candy pink–*Coquille/103*)

3 months: 4 balls A and 1 ball each of the other 3 colors
6 months: 6 balls A and 1 ball each of the other 3 colors
12 months: 6 balls A and 1 ball each of the other 3 colors
5 2-hole pearl buttons
1 pair each #4/3.5mm and #6/4mm knitting needles, or sizes needed to obtain gauge
1 spare needle or stitch holder

Stitches

Stockinette Stitch: See romper instructions.
Garter Stitch: See romper instructions.
Stripe pattern: *Work 2 rows of Garter St in B, 4 rows of Stockinette St in A, 2 rows of Garter St in C, 4 rows of Stockinette St in A, 2 rows of Garter St in D, and 4 rows of Stockinette St in A*. Rep from * to *.

Gauge

23 stitches and 35 rows to a 4"/10cm square knit in Stripe patt on #6/4mm needles.

Take the time to make a gauge swatch, which is especially important if you are substituting the suggested yarn.
If necessary, change needle sizes to obtain the correct gauge.

Making the striped cardigan

The body is worked in a single piece, beg with the right front.

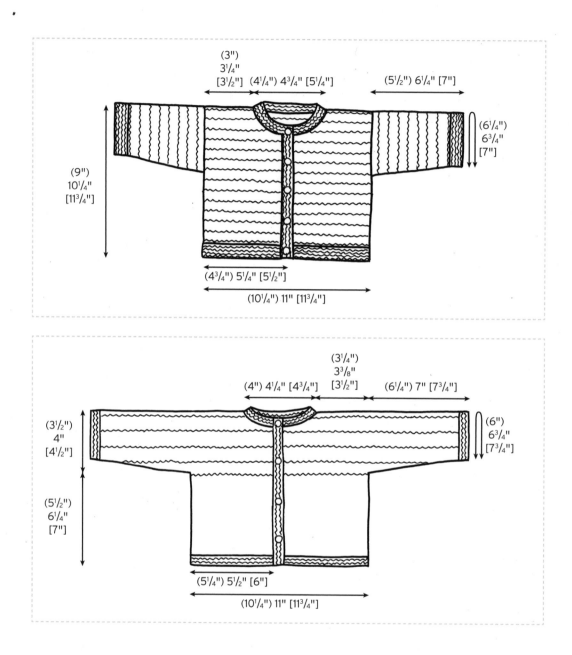

(3")
3¹/₄"
[3¹/₂"] (4¹/₄") 4³/₄" [5¹/₄"]   (5¹/₂") 6¹/₄" [7"]

(6¹/₄")
6³/₄"
[7"]

(9")
10¹/₄"
[11³/₄"]

(4³/₄") 5¹/₄" [5¹/₂"]

(10¹/₄") 11" [11³/₄"]

(3¹/₄")
3³/₈"
[3¹/₂"]
(4") 4¹/₄" [4³/₄"]   (6¹/₄") 7" [7³/₄"]

(6")
6³/₄"
[7³/₄"]

(3¹/₂")
4"
[4¹/₂"]

(5¹/₂")
6¹/₄"
[7"]

(5¹/₄") 5¹/₂" [6"]

(10¹/₄") 11" [11³/₄"]

Using #4/3.5mm needles and A, CO (28) 30 [32] sts and work 8 rows in Garter St, then change to #6/4mm needles and cont in Stripe patt.

When piece measures (7"/18cm) 8¼"/21cm [9½"/24cm], beg shaping neck: BO at neck edge on alt rows, (5) 5 [6] sts, then 4 sts, then 1 st (2) 3 [3] times.

When piece measures (9"/22.5cm) 10¼"/26cm [11¾"/29.5cm]– i.e., at the (13th) 15th [17th] stripe of Garter St–put the rem (17) 18 [19] sts on a spare needle or stitch holder.

Using #4/3.5mm needles and A, CO (28) 30 [32] sts and work the left front in the same way, reversing shapings, then work 1 extra row and CO (26) 28 [30] sts in A for the back neck and work across the (17) 21 [23] sts of the right front from the holder. Cont in Stripe patt but reversing the order of the Garter St stripes (2 rows D, 2 rows C, and 2 rows B) 2 rows C, 2 rows B, and 2 rows D [2 rows B, 2 rows D, and 2 rows C], until (12) 14 [16] of the Garter St stripes are completed, then work 8 rows even in Garter St and BO on the 9th row.

• Sleeves

Using #4/3.5mm needles and A, CO (37) 39 [41] sts and work 8 rows in Garter St, then change to #6/4mm needles and cont in Stripe patt, inc 1 st at each edge of (every 12 rows 3 times) every 8, then every 10 rows alternately 5 times [every 8, then every 10 rows alternately 6 times].

When piece measures (5½"/14cm) 6¼"/16cm [7"/18cm], BO the resulting (43) 49 [53] sts.

Finishing

Using #4/3.5mm needles and A, pick up and K (49) 57 [65] sts along the edge of the left front and work 8 rows in Garter St, then BO.

Work the border on the right front in the same way, forming 4 single-st buttonholes on the 4th row, the 1st buttonhole 2 sts from the RH edge and the rest (11) 13 [15] sts apart.

Using #4/3.5mm needles and A, pick up and K (70) 76 [82] sts around the neck and work a similar border, forming 1 single-st buttonhole 2 sts from the edge on the 2nd row.

Sew on the sleeves (3½"/9cm) 4"/10cm [4¼"/11cm] from the hem, then sew the side and sleeve seams.

Sew on the buttons in line with the buttonholes.

Ecru cardigan ★

Sizes
(3 months) 6 months [12 months]

Materials
Any wool-and-cashmere-blend sport weight yarn, such as Phildar's *Laine et Cachemire* (85% combed wool/15% cashmere; ⅞oz/25g = 65yd/ 60m) in colors: A (ecru–*Écru/032*), B (pale pink–*Rosée/109*), C (pistachio–*Pistache/108*), and D (candy pink–*Coquille/103*)

3 months: 4 balls A and 1oz/25g each of the other 3 colors
6 months: 5 balls A and 1oz/25g each of the other 3 colors
12 months: 6 balls A and 1oz/25g each of the other 3 colors
5 2-hole pearl buttons
1 pair each #4/3.5mm and #6/4mm knitting needles, or sizes needed to obtain gauge
1 spare needle or stitch holder

Stitches
Stockinette Stitch: See romper instructions.
Garter Stitch: See romper instructions.
Stripe pattern: *Work 2 rows of Garter St in B, 6 rows of Stockinette St in A, 2 rows of Garter St in C, 6 rows of Stockinette St in A, 2 rows of Garter St in D, and 6 rows of Stockinette St in A*. Rep from * to *.

Gauges

23 stitches and 31 rows to a 4"/10cm square knit in Stockinette St on #6/4mm needles.

23 stitches and 34 rows to a 4"/10cm square knit in the stripe pattern on #6/4mm needles.

Take the time to make a gauge swatch, which is especially important if you are substituting the suggested yarn.
If necessary, change needle sizes to obtain the correct gauge.

Making the ecru cardigan

The cardigan is worked in a single piece beg with the right front.

Using #4/3.5mm needles and A, CO (30) 32 [35] sts and work 6 rows in Garter St, then change to #6/4mm needles and cont even in Stockinette St.

When piece measures (5¼"/13.5cm) 6"/15.5cm [6¾"/17.5cm], cont working even in the Stripe patt.

When piece measures (5½"/14cm) 6¼"/16cm [7¼"/18cm], beg shaping sleeve: At the LH edge, every alt row, CO (11 sts twice and 10 sts once) 12 sts twice and 13 sts once [14 sts twice and 13 sts once]. Work even on the resulting (62) 69 [76] sts.

When piece measures (8¼"/21cm) 9½"/24cm [10¾"/27cm], beg shaping neck: On RH edge of alt rows, BO (3) 4 [4] sts, then (9) 9 [10] sts.

When piece measures (9"/23cm) 10¼"/26cm [11½"/29.5cm]– i.e., at the (5th Garter St stripe) 5th Garter St stripe + 3 rows Stockinette St [6th Garter St stripe]–you have reached the halfway point. Put the rem (18) 19 [21] sts on a spare needle or stitch holder.

Using #4/3.5mm needles and A, CO (30) 32 [35] sts and work the left front in the same way, reversing shapings. Work 1 more row, then CO (24) 26 [28] sts for the back neck and work across sts of right front from holder. Work even in Stockinette St on the resulting (124) 138 [152] sts until the 2nd half of the sleeves is equal to the 1st half at wrist level, then BO (10) 13 [13] sts at beg of next 2 rows and (11) 12 [14] sts at beg of foll 4 rows.

Work even until the (9th) 10th [11th] Garter St stripe, then cont in Stockinette St with A until piece measures (4¾"/12cm) 5½"/14cm [6¼"/16cm] from the top. Change to #4/3.5mm needles and work 6 rows in Garter St, then BO.

Finishing

Using #4/3.5mm needles and A, pick up and K (51) 58 [65] sts along the right front and work 7 rows in Garter St, then BO.

Work a border on the left front in the same way, making three single-st buttonholes on the 2nd row, the 1st buttonhole at (13) 14 [15] sts from the edge and the others (11) 13 [15] sts apart.

Pick up and K (63) 69 [75] sts around the neck and work 5 rows of Garter St, forming 1 single-st buttonhole 2 sts from end of 2nd row.

Pick up and K (40) 46 [52] sts around the cuffs and work 5 rows of Garter St.

Sew the side and sleeve seams.

Sew buttons on right front in line with buttonholes.

Booties ★★

Sizes
3 months (6 months)

Materials

Any wool-and-cashmere-blend sport weight yarn, such as Phildar's *Laine et Cachemire* (85% combed wool/15% cashmere; ⅞oz/25g = 65yd/60m) in colors: A (ecru–*Écru/032*), B (pale pink–*Rosée/109*), C (pistachio–*Pistache/108*), and D (candy pink–*Coquille/103*).

3 months: ¾oz/20g A and a small amount of the other 3 colors
6 months: 1 ball A and a small amount of the other 3 colors
1 pair #6/4mm knitting needles, or size needed to obtain gauge

Stitches

Stocking Stitch: See romper instructions.
Garter Stitch: See romper instructions.
Left-slanting decrease (SKP): See romper instructions.

Gauge

23 stitches and 31 rows to a 4"/10cm square knit in Stockinette St on #6/4mm needles.

Take the time to make a gauge swatch, which is especially important if you are substituting the suggested yarn.
If necessary, change needle sizes to obtain the correct gauge.

Making the booties

Using #6/4mm needles and A, CO 29 (33) sts and work in Garter St, inc on alt rows, 1 st at each end and 1 st on either side of the center st 4 times. Work 10 rows on the resulting 45 (50) sts, then beg the upper part of the bootie: K18 (20), *K8 (9), SKP, turn. P8 (9), SKP, turn*. Rep from * to * until 13 (14) sts rem unworked on either side, then cut the yarn. Transfer the 13 (14) sts rem on the RH needle to the LH needle and work 8 rows in Stockinette St on these 35 (38) sts. Change to Garter St and knit 4 rows B, 2 rows C, and 2 rows D, then BO. Pick up and K 1 loop from each st on 5th row of Garter St, counting down from the upper part of the bootie, and K 1 row, BO as you go.

Sew the back and sole of the bootie.

Make the 2nd bootie in the same way.

precious layette

Simple and chic, for birthdays and holidays, this immaculate white outfit would be lovely worn over a pretty shirt with a lace collar.

Jacket ★

Sizes
(Newborn) 3 months [6 months]

Materials
Any lamb's wool-and-acrylic-blend fingering weight yarn, such as Phildar's *Lambswool* (51% lamb's wool/49% acryli; 1¾oz/50g = 145yd/134m) in white (*Blanc/010*)
Newborn: 2 balls
3 months: 3 balls
6 months: 3 balls
5 small white 2-hole buttons
1 pair #3/3mm needles, or size needed to obtain gauge
5 #3/3mm double-pointed needles

Stitches
Stockinette Stitch: K 1 row, P 1 row.
Picot edging: *Row 1:* K1, *K2tog, yo*, rep from * to *, K1.
Row 2: P.

Gauge
26 stitches and 35 rows to a 4"/10cm square knit in Stockinette St on #3/3mm needles.

Take the time to make a gauge swatch, which is especially important if you are substituting the suggested yarn. If necessary, change needle sizes to obtain the correct gauge.

Making the jacket

• Back
Using #3/3mm needles CO (68) 74 [78] sts and work (6"/15cm) 6¾"/17cm [7½"/19cm] in Stockinette St, then beg shaping armholes: BO 3 sts at beg of next 2 rows, 2 sts at beg of next 2 rows, then 1 st at beg of next 4 rows.

When piece measures (9"/23cm) 10¼"/26cm [11½"/29cm], beg shaping neck: On next row, BO the (20) 22 [24] center sts and finish each side separately. Beg at neck edge, BO 2 sts on next row, then work even until piece measures (9½"/24cm) 10¾"/27cm [11¾"/30cm], then BO the rem (15) 17 [18] sts.

• Left front
Using #3/3mm needles, CO (34) 37 [39] sts and work even in Stockinette St until piece measures (6"/15cm) 6¾"/17cm [7½"/19cm], then beg shaping armhole: Beg at armhole edge on alt rows, BO 3 sts, then 2 sts then 1 st twice. Cont working even until piece measures (7¾"/20cm) 9"/23cm [10"/26cm], then beg shaping neck: Beg at neck edge on alt rows, BO (4) 5 [5] sts

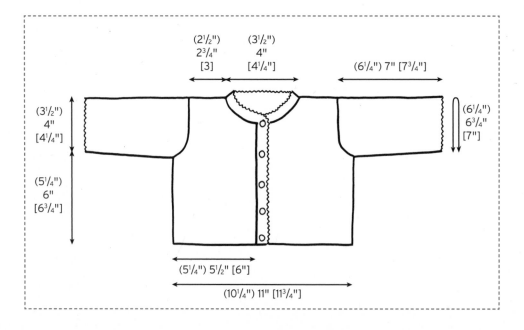

once, then 3 sts once, 2 sts twice, and 1 st (once) once [twice]. Cont even until work measures (9½"/24cm) 10¾"/27cm [11¾"/30cm], then BO the rem (15) 17 [18] sts.

• **Right front**
Work as for left front, reversing shapings.

• **Sleeves**
Using #3/3mm needles, CO (42) 44 [48] sts and work 6 rows in Stockinette St, then 2 rows of Picot edging. Cont in Stockinette St, inc 1 st at each end of (every 12 rows 3 times) every 10, then every 12 rows alternately 4 times [every 10 rows 5 times].

When piece measures (6"/15cm) 6¾"/17cm [7½"/19cm], BO (3) 3 [4] sts at beg of next 2 rows, 2 sts at beg of next 4 rows, 3 sts at beg of next 2 rows, (7) 8 [9] sts at beg of next 2 rows, then BO the rem (14) 16 [18] sts.

Finishing

Sew the side and sleeve seams.

Turn up a ¾"/2cm hem at the bottom of the back and both fronts.

Using #3/3mm dpn, pick up and K (44) 50 [58] sts along the right front edge, then 4 sts at the corner of the neck, (60) 66 [72] sts around the neck, 4 sts at the corner, and (44) 50 [58] sts down the left front edge. Work 6 rows in Stockinette St on the resulting (156) 174 [196] sts, on the 2nd row making five 2-st buttonholes on the right front, the 1st buttonhole at (4) 2 [2] sts

from the bottom and the others (8) 10 [12] sts apart, then work 2 rows of Picot edging, foll by 6 rows in Stockinette St, making 5 more matching buttonholes on the 5th row. BO loosely.

Sew the seams of the sleeves and set in the armholes.

Fold back the ends of cuffs along the picot edge and sl st to WS.

Fold back the border in the same way, superimposing the buttonholes and sewing the edges of the buttonholes together.

Sew the buttons onto the left front in line with the buttonholes.

Bubble suit ★★

Sizes
(Newborn) 3 months [6 months]

Materials
Any lamb's wool-and-acrylic-blend fingering weight yarn, such as Phildar's *Lambswool* (51% lamb's wool/49% acrylic; 1¾oz/50g = 145yd/134m) in white (*Blanc/010*)
Newborn: 3 balls
3 months: 3 balls
6 months: 4 balls
1 pair each #2/2.5mm and #3/3mm knitting needles, or sizes needed to obtain gauge
1 spare needle or stitch holder
2 small white 2-hole buttons

Stitches
Single Rib: *K1, P1*, rep from * to *.
Stockinette Stitch: See jacket instructions.
Picot edging: See jacket instructions.

Gauge
See jacket instructions.

Making the bubble suit

• **Back**
Begin with the left leg.

Using #2/2.5mm needles, CO (36) 39 [41] sts and work 2"/5cm in Single Rib.

Change to #3/3mm needles and cont in Stockinette St. On next row, inc 16 sts evenly along the row, then inc 1 st at RH edge of the 4th row, then 2 sts at RH edge of 8th row. Put the sts on a spare needle or stitch holder.

Work the right leg in the same way, reversing shapings, then CO 5 sts for the crotch and work across the sts of left leg from holder. Cont working even on rem (115) 121 [125] sts.**

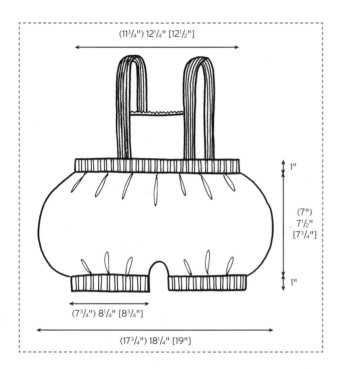

(11³/₄") 12¹/₄" [12¹/₂"]

1"

(7")
7¹/₂"
[7³/₄"]

1"

(7³/₄") 8¹/₄" [8³/₄"]

(17³/₄") 18¹/₄" [19"]

Turn under and sl st a 1"/2.5cm hem at the cuffs and waist.

Fold back the top of the bib to form the picot edge and sl st it to WS, then sew the suspenders along the sides.

Sew the bib to the center front under the ribbing at the waist.

Sew on 2 buttons 2³/₄"/7cm apart, equidistant from center back.

Booties ★★

Sizes
Newborn [3 months]

Materials
Any lamb's wool-and-acrylic-blend fingering weight yarn, such as Phildar's *Lambswool* (51% lamb's wool/49% acrylic; 1³/₄oz/50g = 145yd/134m) in white (*Blanc/010*)
Newborn: 1oz/30 g
3 months: 1¹/₄oz/35g
1 pair each #2/2.5mm and #3/3mm knitting needles, or sizes needed to obtain gauge
3 spare needles or stitch holders

When piece measures (9"/23cm) 9¹/₂"/24cm [9³/₄"/25cm], in order to inc fullness, work across the next row to within 11 sts of the end, then turn. Work the next 5 rows in the same way, leaving 11 more sts at the end every time. On next row work to the end of the row, then change to #2/2.5mm needles and work 2"/5cm in Single Rib, dec (38) 40 [42] sts evenly along the 1st row, then BO loosely.

• Front
Work as for back to **.

When piece measures (9"/23cm) 9¹/₂"/24cm [9³/₄"/25cm], change to #2/2.5mm needles and work 2"/5cm in Single Rib, dec (38) 40 [42] sts evenly along the 1st row, then BO loosely.

• Bib
Using #3/3mm needles, CO (24) 26 [28] sts and work (3¹/₄"/8cm) 3¹/₂"/8.5cm [3³/₄"/9cm] in Stockinette St, then 2 rows of the Picot edging, 5 rows in Stockinette St, and BO loosely.

• Suspenders
Using #2/2.5mm needles, CO 11 sts and work in Single Rib. When piece measures (13¹/₂"/34cm) 15"/38cm [16¹/₂"/42cm], make a single-st buttonhole in the center of the suspender, then to make the point, keeping in rib, SK2P on the 3 center sts of every alt row twice, then every row twice, then BO the rem 3 sts in rib.

Finishing
Sew the side seams.

Stitches

Stockinette Stitch: See jacket instructions.
Single Rib: See bloomers instructions.
Garter Stitch: K every row.
Left-slanting decrease (SKP): Sl 1 knitwise, K1, PSSO.
Double decrease (SK2P): Sl 1, K2tog, PSSO.

Gauge

See jacket instructions.

Making the booties

Using #2/2.5mm needles, CO 47 [51] sts and work 2½"/6cm [3¼"/8cm] in Single Rib.

Change to #3/3mm needles and beg the upper part of the bootie: On next row K31 (34) sts, then put rem 16 [17] sts on a spare needle or stitch holder. Turn work and purl the 15 [17] center sts, dec 4 sts evenly across them, then put the rem 16 [17] sts on a spare needle or stitch holder. Cont in Stockinette St on rem sts of upper part of the bootie until it measures 1⅜"/3.5cm [1½"/4cm], then knit 4 rows in Garter St, cut the yarn, and put sts on a spare needle or stitch holder.

Pick up the 16 [17] sts of RH side and knit them, dec 4 sts evenly across them, then pick up and K 10 [11] sts along the RH edge of the upper part of the bootie, knit across the 11 [13] center sts from the holder, pick up and K 10 [11] sts along the LH edge and knit the 16 [17] sts rem on the other side, dec 4 sts evenly across them. K 8 [10] rows in Garter St on the resulting 55 [61] sts.

To shape the sole, change to #2/2.5mm needles and cont in Garter St as foll: *Row 1:* K4 [5], K3tog, K14 [15], SKP, K7 [9], K3tog, K14 [15], SK2P, K4 [5]. *Row 2:* K. *Row 3:* K3 [4], K3tog, K12 [13], SKP, K5 [7], K3tog, K12 [13], SK2P, K3 [4], lining up the decs with those on the previous row. *Row 4:* K. *Row 5:* As Row 3. *Row 6:* K. *Row 7:* As Row 3. BO the rem 23 [29] sts.

Sew the sole and halfway up the back on WS, then sew top half on RS to form the turnover.

multicolored merry-go-round

multicolored merry-go-round

An array of sparkling colors for a baby in top form!

Pants ★★★

Sizes

(3 months) 6 months [12 months]

Materials

Any polyamide-combed-wool-acrylic blend bulky weight yarn, such as Phildar's *Partner* (50% polyamide/25% combed wool/25% acrylic; 1¾oz/50 = 72yd/66m) in colors: A (purple–*Mûre/106*), B (olive–*Olive/013*), C (bright pink–*Pétunia/016*), D (orange–*Potiron/012*), and E (turquoise–*Perse/015*)

3 months: 2 balls of A and 1 ball each of the other 4 colors
6 months: 3 balls of A and 1 ball each of the other 4 colors
12 months: 3 balls of A and 1 ball each of the other 4 colors
elastic cord
1 pair each #7/4.5mm and #8/5mm knitting needles, or sizes needed to obtain gauge
1 spare needle or stitch holder

Stitches

Single Rib: *K1, P1*, rep from * to *.
Stockinette Stitch: K 1 row, P 1 row.
Garter Stitch: K every row.
Jacquard Stockinette Stitch: Follow the chart, twisting yarns together at each color change. After the last row, beg again with the 1st row.

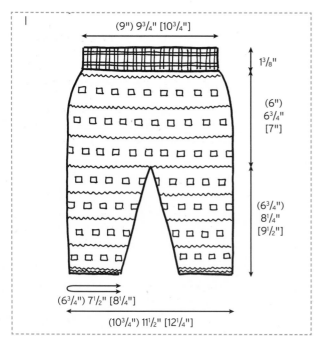

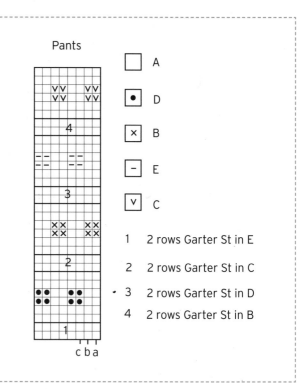

Pants

☐	A
⊡	D
⊠	B
⊟	E
⊻	C

1	2 rows Garter St in E
2	2 rows Garter St in C
· 3	2 rows Garter St in D
4	2 rows Garter St in B

c b a

Gauge

17 stitches and 24 rows to a 4"/10cm square knit in Jacquard Stockinette St patt on #8/5mm needles.

Take the time to make a gauge swatch, which is especially important if you are substituting the suggested yarn.
If necessary, change needle sizes to obtain the correct gauge.

Making the pants

The pants are knit in one piece, beg with the right leg.

Using #8/5mm needles and D, CO (29) 32 [36] sts and work in Jacquard Stockinette St patt, beg at a on the chart, and inc 1 st at each end of (every 4 rows 9 times) every 4 rows 5 times, then every 6 rows 4 times [every 6 rows 9 times].

When piece measures (6¾"/17cm) 8¼"/21cm [9½"/24cm], BO 2 sts at beg of next 2 rows and 1 st at beg of next 4 rows, then put the rem (39) 42 [46] sts on a spare needle or stitch holder.

Work the left leg in the same way, beg the Jacquard Stockinette St patt at (b) c [c], then work across the right leg sts from the holder and cont on resulting (78) 84 [92] sts until piece measures (12½"/32cm) 14½"/37cm [16½"/42cm]–i.e., after 2 rows in Stockinette St in A–change to #7/4.5mm needles and Single Rib and work 2 rows B, 1 row C, 2 rows D, 1 row C, 1 row E, then BO in rib.

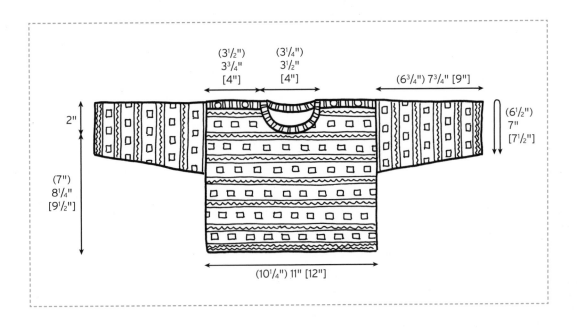

The diagram shows the sweater with the following measurements:

- (3½") 3¾" [4"]
- (3¼") 3½" [4"]
- (6¾") 7¾" [9"]
- 2"
- (6½") 7" [7½"]
- (7") 8¼" [9½"]
- (10¼") 11" [12"]

Finishing

Sew the back and leg seams.

Thread a few rows of elastic cord through the ribbing.

Sweater ★★★

Sizes

(3 months) 6 months [12 months]

Materials

Any polyamide-combed-wool-acrylic blend bulky weight yarn, such as Phildar's *Partner* (50% polyamide/25% combed wool/25% acrylic; 1¾oz/50 = 72yd/66m) in colors: A (purple–*Mûre/106*), B (olive–*Olive/013*), C (bright pink–*Pétunia/016*), D (orange–*Potiron/012*), and E (turquoise–*Perse/015*)
For all sizes: 1 ball each of the 5 colors
4 bright pink 4-hole buttons
1 pair each #7/4.5mm and #8/5mm knitting needles, or sizes needed to obtain gauge

Stitches

Single Rib: See pants instructions.
Stockinette Stitch: See pants instructions.
Garter Stitch: See pants instructions.
Jacquard Stockinette Stitch: See pants instructions.

Gauge

See pants instructions.

Making the sweater

• Back

Using #8/5mm needles and D, CO (44) 48 [52] sts and work even in Jacquard Stockinette St patt, foll the chart.**

When piece measures (7¾"/20cm) 9"/23cm [10¾"/27cm], beg shaping neck: BO the (14) 16 [18] center sts of next row and finish each side separately.

When piece measures (8"/21cm) 9½"/24cm [11¼"/28cm], beg shaping shoulder: Change to #7/4.5mm needles and E, and work ⅝"/1.5cm in Single Rib on the rem (15) 16 [17] sts, then BO in rib.

• Front

Work as for back to **.

When piece measures (7"/17.5cm) 8¼"/21cm [9¾"/24.5cm]– i.e., foll 2 rows in Garter St–beg shaping neck: BO the (6) 8 [10] center sts of next row and finish each side separately. Beg at neck edge, dec 3 sts at beg of next row, work 1 row, then dec 1 st at beg of foll row.

When piece measures (8¼"/21cm) 9¾"/24.5cm [11"/28cm], beg shaping shoulder: Change to #7/4.5mm needles and E, and work ⅝"/1.5cm in Single Rib, making a single-st buttonhole on the 1st row 7 sts from the neck edge, then BO in rib.

Sweater

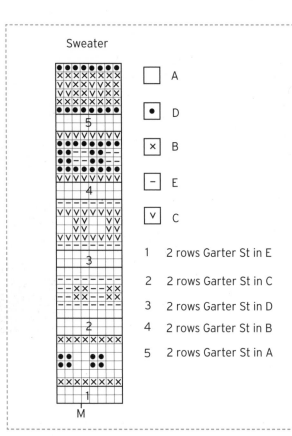

A

• D

× B

- E

v C

1   2 rows Garter St in E

2   2 rows Garter St in C

3   2 rows Garter St in D

4   2 rows Garter St in B

5   2 rows Garter St in A

• Sleeves

Using #8/5mm needles and D, CO (28) 30 [32] sts and work in
Jacquard Stockinette St patt, making sure point M on the chart
is in the center of the work, and inc 1 st at each end of (every
8 rows twice, then every 10 rows twice) every 8 rows 3 times,
then every 10 rows twice [every 8 rows 6 times].

When piece measures (6¾"/17cm) 7¾"/20cm [9"/23cm],
BO the resulting (36) 40 [44] sts.

Finishing

Using #7/4.5mm needles and C, pick up and K (25) 27 [29] sts
around back neck and work 2 rows in Single Rib, then BO in rib.

Using #7/4.5mm needles and C, pick up and K (31) 33 [35] sts
around front neck and work 2 rows in Single Rib, making a
single-st buttonhole 2 sts from each end of 1st row, then BO
in rib.

Overlap the rib band at the shoulders and join at the sleeve
edge, then set in the sleeves and sew the sleeve and side seams.

Sew the buttons onto the shoulders of the back in line with the
buttonholes.

Hat ★★

Sizes
3/6 months (12 months)

Materials
Any polyamide-combed-wool-acrylic blend bulky weight yarn,
such as Phildar's *Partner* (50% polyamide/25% combed
wool/25% acrylic; 1¾oz/50 = 72yd/66m) in colors: A (purple–
Mûre/106), B (olive–*Olive/013*), C (bright pink–*Pétunia/016*),
D (orange–*Potiron/012*), E (turquoise–*Perse/015*), and F (red–
Pavot/102)

For both sizes: 1 ball A and small amount of other 5 colors
1 pair #8/5mm knitting needles, or size needed to obtain gauge

Stitches
Stockinette Stitch: See pants instructions.
Garter Stitch: See pants instructions.
Jacquard Stockinette Stitch: See pants instructions.
Jacquard figures: Worked in Stockinette St, following the chart.
Left-slanting decrease (SKP): Sl 1 knitwise, K1, PSSO.
Double decrease (SK2P): Sl 1 knitwise, K2tog, PSSO.

Gauge
See pants instructions.

Making the hat
Using #8/5mm needles and A, CO 66 (74) sts and work 2 rows in
Garter St, then cont in Jacquard figures, working 1 st in A, then
1 boy figure in E, 1 girl figure in C, 1 boy figure in B, 1 girl figure in
D, 1 boy figure in E, 1 girl figure in C, 1 boy figure in B, 1 girl figure
in D, plus 1 boy figure in E *for size 12 months only*, then 1 st in A.

After the last row of the chart, work 4 rows of Stockinette
St in A, then 2 rows of Garter St in F and cont in Jacquard
Stockinette St patt, starting at the 19th row of the sweater chart.

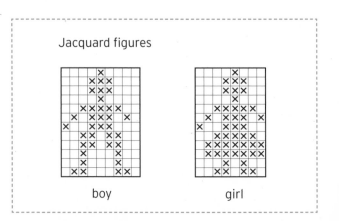

Jacquard figures

boy   girl

At the 5th row of the chart, SKP 8 (9) times, the 1st dec at 4 sts in from the edge and the rest 6 sts apart. Work 3 more rows, then on the foll row SK2P 8 (9) times, the 1st dec at 3 sts in from edge and the rest 4 sts apart. Work 1 row, then on the next row SK2P 8 (9) times, lining the decs up with those on the previous rows. Then work 3 rows, foll by a row with 4 (5) SK2P, the 1st dec at 1 st in from the edge and the rest 3 sts apart. Work 8 more rows, then on next row SKP 4 times, the 1st dec at 2 sts in from the edge and the rest 2 sts apart.

Cut the yarn and pass it through the rem 14 (15) sts, then pull it tight and fasten off.

Sew the hat.

Make 2 braids in C and 2 in D, using three 4"/10cm strands of yarn, then make a knot at each end. Pass 1 braid under the 3 sts at the top of the head of each girl figure, contrasting the colors, and anchor them with a few sts.

Jacket ★★★

Sizes
(6 months) 12 months [18 months]

Materials
Any polyamide-combed-wool-acrylic blend bulky weight yarn, such as Phildar's *Partner* (50% polyamide/25% combed wool/ 25% acrylic; 1 ³⁄₄oz/50g = 72yd/66m) in colors: A (purple– Mûre/106), B (olive–*Olive/013*), C (bright pink–*Pétunia/016*), D (orange–*Potiron/012*), E (turquoise–*Perse/015*), F (red– *Pavot/102*), andg (plum– *Prune/100*)
6 months: 2 balls G, 1 ball A, and small amount of other 5 colors
12 months: 3 balls G, 2 balls A, and small amount of other 5 colors
18 months: 3 balls G, 2 balls A, and small amount of other 5 colors
1 pair #8/5mm knitting needles, or size needed to obtain gauge
3 red 4-hole buttons

Stitches
Stockinette Stitch: See pants instructions.
Garter Stitch: See pants instructions.
Jacquard figures: See hat instructions.

Gauge
16 stitches and 22 rows to a 4"/10cm square knit in Stockinette St on #8/5mm needles.

Take the time to make a gauge swatch, which is especially important if you are substituting the suggested yarn.
If necessary, change needle sizes to obtain the correct gauge.

Making the jacket

• Back
Using #8/5mm needles and A, CO (46) 50 [54] sts and work 2 rows in Garter St, then cont in Jacquard figure patt. K (1) 1 [3] sts in A, then work 1 boy figure in E, 1 girl figure in C, 1 boy figure in B, 1 girl figure in D, 1 boy figure in E, 1 girl figure in C, K (1) 1 [3] in A (*for size 6 months*, work the 8 sts of the chart for the 1st and last motifs and only the 7 first sts for the 4 center motifs). After the last row of the chart, work 4 rows in Stockinette St in A, then 2 rows in Garter St in F and cont in Stockinette St in G, dec 1 st at each end of the 5th row.

When piece measures (4³⁄₄"/12cm) 5½"/14cm [6¼"/16cm], BO 2 sts at beg of next two rows for armholes and cont even until piece measures (8³⁄₄"/22cm) 9³⁄₄"/25cm [11"/28cm], then beg shaping neck: BO the (14) 16 [18] center sts of next row, and finish each side separately.

When piece measures (9"/23cm) 10¼"/26cm [11½"/29cm], BO the rem (13) 14 [15] sts.

• Right front
Using #8/5mm needles and A, CO (23) 26 [28] sts and work 2 rows in Garter St, then cont in Jacquard figure patt: K (1) 1 [2] sts in A, then work 1 girl figure in C, 1 boy figure in B, 1 girl figure in D, K (1) 1 [2] sts in A (*for size 6 months*, work 7 sts only for each of the 3 motifs). After the last row in the chart, work 4 rows in Stockinette St in A and 2 rows in Garter St in F, then cont in Stockinette St in G, dec 1 st at the LH edge of the 5th row.

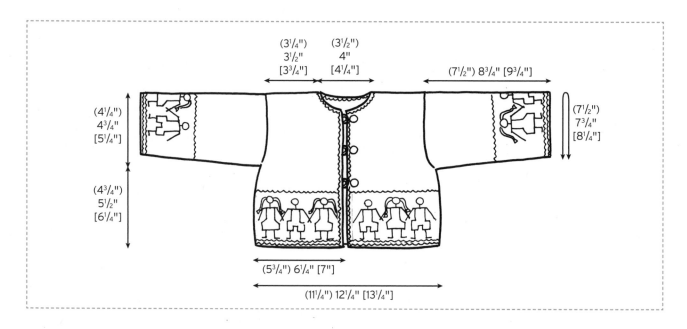

(3¼") 3½" [3¾"] (3½") 4" [4¼"] (7½") 8¾" [9¾"]

(4¼") 4¾" [5¼"] (7½") 7¾" [8¼"]

(4¾") 5½" [6¼"]

(5¾") 6¼" [7"]

(11¼") 12¼" [13¼"]

When piece measures (4¾"/12cm) 5½"/14cm [6¼"/16cm] from beg, BO 2 sts at armhole edge.

When piece measures (7¾"/20cm) 9"/23cm [10¼"/26cm], beg shaping neck: Working from RH edge, BO (4) 5 [5] sts at beg of 1st row, (2) 3 [3] sts on 3rd row, and (1) 1 [2] sts on 5th row.

When piece measures (9"/23cm) 10¼"/26cm [11½"/29cm], BO the rem (13) 14 [15] sts for the shoulder.

• Left front

Work as for right front, reversing shapings.

For Jacquard figures, work 1 boy figure in B, 1 girl figure in D, and 1 boy figure in E.

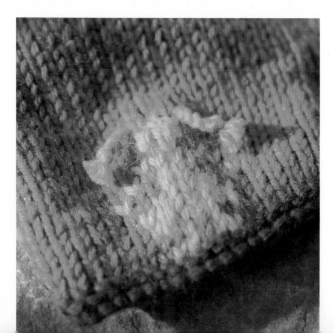

• Right sleeve

Using #8/5mm needles and A, CO (30) 32 [34] sts and work 2 rows in Garter St, then cont in Jacquard figure patt, inc 1 st at each end of (every 12 rows 3 times) every 14 rows 3 times [every 12 rows 4 times].

Work (3) 4 [5] sts in A, then 1 boy figure in E, 1 girl figure in C, 1 boy figure in B, and (3) 4 [5] sts in A. After the last row of the chart, work 4 rows in Stockinette St in A and 2 rows in Garter St in F, then cont in Stockinette St in G.

When piece measures (7½"/19cm) 8¾"/22cm [9¾"/25cm], BO the rem (36) 38 [42] sts.

• Left sleeve

Work as for right sleeve, making 1 girl figure in D, 1 boy figure in E, and 1 girl figure in C.

Finishing

Sew the shoulder seams.

Using F, pick up and K (34) 39 [44] sts along the right front edge, then BO on next row as you knit. Rep along left front.

Pick up and K (38) 42 [46] sts around the neck and work the same border.

Set in the sleeves and sew the sleeve and side seams.

On the right front edge make 3 button loops with 1 strand of F, 1 at the neck border, 1 level with the rows of Garter St in F, and 1 equidistant between the 2.

Sew the buttons onto the left front in line with the loops.

Make 3 braids in D and 3 braids in C using three 4"/10cm strands of yarn, then make a knot at each end. Pass 1 braid under the 3 sts at the top of the head of each girl figure on the back and both fronts, contrasting the colors, and anchor them with a few sts.

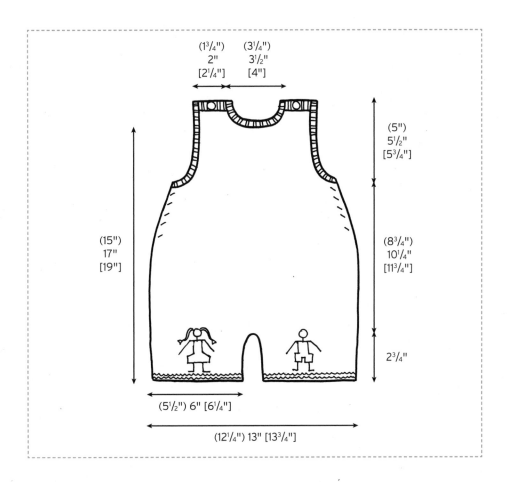

(1¾") 2" [2¼"] (3¼") 3½" [4"]

(5") 5½" [5¾"]

(15") 17" [19"]

(8¾") 10¼" [11¾"]

2¾"

(5½") 6" [6¼"]

(12¼") 13" [13¾"]

Overalls ★

Sizes
(6 months) 12 months [18 months]

Materials
Any polyamide-combed-wool-acrylic blend bulky weight yarn, such as Phildar's *Partner* (50% polyamide,/25% combed wool/25% acrylic; 1¾oz/50g = 72yd/66m) in colors: A (purple–*Mûre/106*), B (olive–*Olive/013*), C (bright pink–*Pétunia/016*), D (orange–*Potiron/012*), E (turquoise–*Perse/015*), F (red–*Pavot/102*), and G (plum–*Prune/100*)
6 months: 4 balls F and small amount of other 6 colors
12 months: 6 balls F and small amount of other 6 colors
18 months: 7 balls F and small amount of other 6 colors
1 pair each #7/4.5mm and #8/5mm knitting needles, or sizes needed to obtain gauge
1 spare needle or stitch holder
2 purple 4-hole buttons

Stitches
Stockinette Stitch: See pants instructions.
Garter Stitch: See pants instructions.
Single Rib: See pants instructions.
Left-slanting decrease (SKP): See hat instructions.
Jacquard figures: See hat instructions.

Gauge
See jacket instructions.

Making the overalls

• Back
Beg with the left leg.
Using #7/4.5mm needles and G, CO (22) 24 [26] sts and work 2 rows of Garter St in A. Change to #8/5mm needles and F and work in Jacquard figure patt, beg with a girl figure in D at (9) 10 [11] sts in from the edge of 1st row. Cont until piece measures 2"/5cm. At RH edge of work, inc 1 st on next 2 alt rows, then put the resulting (24) 26 [28] sts on a spare needle or stitch holder.

Work the right leg in the same way, reversing shapings and working a boy figure in E, then CO 1 st for the crotch and work across the sts of left leg from the holder. Cont on resulting (49) 53 [57] sts.

When piece measures (8¼"/21cm) 9¾"/25cm [11½"/29cm], at 1 st in from the edge, dec 1 st at each end of every 4th row 5 times (use SKP to dec on RH edge and K2tog to dec on LH edge).

When piece measures (11½"/29cm) 13"/33cm [14½"/37cm], beg shaping armholes: BO 3 sts at beg of next 2 rows, 2 sts at beg of next 2 rows, and 1 st at beg of next 2 rows.

When piece measures (15"/38cm) 17"/43cm [19"/48cm], beg shaping neck: BO the (7) 9 [11] center sts of next row and finish each side separately. At neck edge of alt rows, BO 2 sts, then 1 st, then change to #7/4.5mm needles and work ⅝"/1.5cm in Single Rib on the rem (7) 8 [9] sts and BO in rib.

- **Front**

Work as for back, working 1 girl figure in C and 1 boy figure in B, and forming a single-st buttonhole in the center of the 2nd row of rib.

Finishing

Using #7/4.5mm needles and F, pick up and K (29) 31 [33] sts around the front neck and work 2 rows in Single Rib, then BO in rib. Work similar border on back neck.

Sew the leg seams.

Using #7/4.5mm needles and F, pick up and K (53) 57 [61] sts around RH armhole and work 2 rows in Single Rib, then BO in rib. Work similar border around LH armhole.

Make 1 braid in D and 1 braid in C using three 4"/10cm strands of yarn, then make a knot at each end. Pass 1 braid under the 3 sts at the top of the head of each girl figure, contrasting the colors, and anchor them with a few sts.

Sew the buttons onto the back shoulders.

Booties ★★

Sizes
3/6 months (12 months)

Materials
Any polyamide-combed-wool-acrylic blend bulky weight yarn, such as Phildar's *Partner* (50% polyamide/25% combed wool/25% acrylic; 1¾oz/50g = 72yd/66m) in colors: A (purple–*Mûre/106*), B (olive–*Olive/013*), C (bright pink–*Pétunia/016*), D (orange–*Potiron/012*), and E (turquoise–*Perse/015*)
3 months: ¾oz/20g A and small amount of other 5 colors
6 months: 1oz/30g A and small amount of other 5 colors
1 pair #8/5mm knitting needles, or size needed to obtain gauge
1 spare needle or stitch holder

Stitches
Stockinette Stitch: See pants instructions.
Garter Stitch: See pants instructions.
Jacquard Stockinette Stitch: See pants instructions.
Jacquard figures: See hat instructions.

Gauge
See pants instructions.

Making the booties
Beg with the sole.

Using #8/5mm needles and A, CO 9 sts and work 4 rows in Stockinette St, then 1 boy figure in E, then 3 (5) rows in Stockinette St, then BO.

Make a 2nd sole working a girl figure in D.

For the upper part of the bootie: Using #8/5mm needles and A, CO 38 (42) sts and work 1 row C, 1 row D, 2 rows alternating 2 sts in D with 2 sts in E, 1 row D, and 1 row C, then beg shaping upper part of the bootie. Cut the yarn and put 15 (17) sts at each end on a spare needle or stitch holder and, using A, cont on the 8 center sts only. K7 then sl the last st, K the 1st of the sts from the holder and PSSO. Turn work, *sl 1, P6, sl the last st, P 1st st from the holder and PSSO, turn work, sl 1, K6, sl the last st, K 1st st from the holder and PSSO*, rep from * to * until 11(12) sts rem on holder on each side. Cut yarn. Using A, beg again at RH edge, working the 11(12) sts of RH side, then the 8 sts of the upper part of the bootie and the 11 (12) sts of LH side. Work 1 row A, 2 rows alternating 2 sts B and 2 sts A, 2 rows A, 2 rows in Garter St in D, then change to A and purl next row, BO as you go.

Make another bootie in the same way.

Finishing
Sew the back seam of the bootie, then oversew the sole to it with a strand of A.

Make 1 braid with three 4"/10cm strands of C, then make a knot at each end. Pass the braid under the 3 sts at the top of the head of the girl figure and anchor with a few sts.

Make 2 braided cords with three 14"/35cm strands of C, then make a knot at each end. Pass the cords under the st at either end of the last row of the upper part of the bootie.

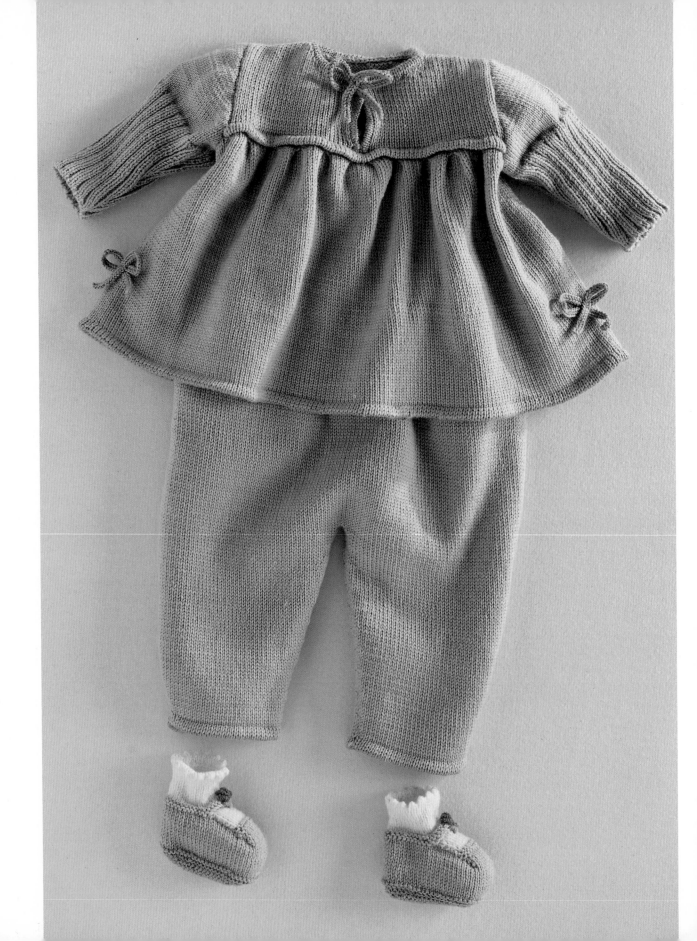

a perfect little girl

a perfect little girl

Soft pastel shades for these classic patterns are enhanced by delightful details.

Pants ★

Sizes

(3 months) 6 months [12 months]

Materials

Any 100% wool fingering weight yarn, such as Bouton d'Or's *Baby Superwash* (100% wool; 1¾oz/50g = 219yd/200m) in colors: A (pale pink–*Rosée/513*) and B (silver gray–*Glacier/231*)

3 months: 3 balls A and a small amount of B
6 months: 3 balls A and a small amount of B
12 months: 4 balls A and a small amount of B
(16"/40cm) 17"/44cm [18"/46cm] of ¾"/2cm wide elastic
1 pair #3/3mm knitting needles, or size needed to obtain gauge
1 spare needle or stitch holder

Stitches

Stockinette Stitch: K 1 row, P 1 row.
Make One (M1): Pick up and K or P loop between last st knitted and next st on LH needle.

Gauge

30 stitches and 40 rows to a 4"/10cm square knit in Stockinette St on #3/3mm needles.

Take the time to make a gauge swatch, which is especially important if you are substituting the suggested yarn.
If necessary, change needle sizes to obtain the correct gauge.

Making the pants

• Front

Begin with the right leg.

Using #3/3mm needles and A, CO (30) 33 [36] sts and work in Stockinette St: 3 rows A, 2 rows B, 3 rows A, then make the hem on the next row by knitting each st from the needle tog with the corresponding loop from the CO row. Cont in A, M1 at RH edge of (every 6 rows 10 times) every 6, then every 8 rows alternately 10 times [every 8 rows 10 times]. On LH edge, M1 at beg of alt rows 10 times for all 3 sizes.

When piece measures (7"/18cm) 8¼"/21cm [9½"/24cm], put the resulting (50) 53 [56] sts on a spare needle or stitch holder.

Work the left leg in the same way, reversing shapings, then work across the sts of right leg from holder and cont working even on the resulting (100) 106 [112] sts until piece measures (13¾"/35cm) 15½"/39cm [17"/43cm]. On next row, dec (16) 17 [18] sts as foll: K4, *K2tog, K4*, rep from * to * 16 times. Cont working even on rem (84) 89 [94] sts for 2½"/6cm, then BO.

• Back

Work as for front.

Finishing

Sew the leg and side seams.

Turn up a 1¼"/3cm hem at the top of the pants and thread the elastic through the waistband casing.

Swing top ★★

Sizes

(3 months) 6 months [12 months]

Materials

Any 100% wool fingering weight yarn, such as Bouton d'Or's *Baby Superwash* (100% wool; 1¾oz/50g = 219yd/200m) in colors: A (pale pink–*Rosée/513*) and B (silver gray–*Glacier/231*)

3 months: 3 balls A and a small amount of B
6 months: 4 balls A and a small amount of B
12 months: 4 balls A and a small amount of B
1 snap fastener
1 pair #3/3mm knitting needles, or size needed to obtain gauge
1 set #3/3mm double-pointed needles
1 spare needle or stitch holder

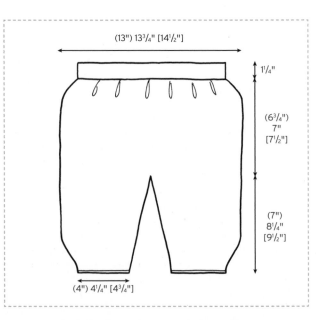

(13") 13¾" [14½"]
1¼"
(6¾") 7" [7½"]
(7") 8¼" [9½"]
(4") 4¼" [4¾"]

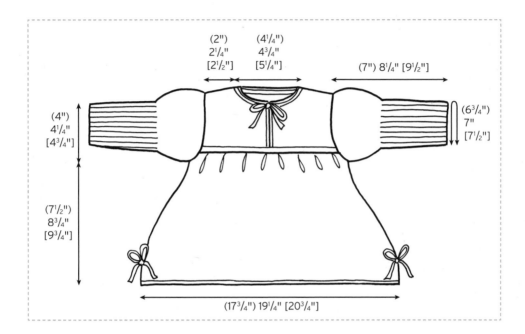

Stitches

Stockinette Stitch: See pants instructions.
Double Rib: *K2, P2*, rep from * to *.

Gauge

See pants instructions.

Making the swing top

• Front

Using #3/3mm needles and A, CO (134) 146 [158] sts and work in Stockinette St: 3 rows A, 2 rows B, 3 rows A, then make a hem on the next row by knitting 1 st from the needle tog with corresponding loop from the CO row. Cont working even in A until piece measures (7½"/19cm) 8¾"/22cm [9¾"/25cm], then beg shaping armholes: BO 3 sts at beg of next 2 rows, 2 sts at beg of next 2 rows, and 1 st at beg of next 2 rows.

When piece measures (7¾"/20cm) 9"/23cm [10¼"/26cm], dec (60) 66 [72] sts on the next row as foll: K1, *sl 3 sts on a #3/3mm dpn and place behind the work. K1 st from LH needle tog with 1 st from dpn 3 times, sl 3 sts on dpn and place in front of work, K 1 st from dpn tog with 1 st from LH needle *. Rep from * to * (10) 11 [12] times in all, K last st.

Work 9 more rows in Stockinette St, then make the pleat on the next row: K each st from LH needle tog with corresponding st on 9th previous row.**

Work 1 more row, then on next row BO the 2 center sts for the opening and finish each side separately.

Work even until piece measures (2¼"/5.5cm) 2½"/6.5cm [3"/7.5cm] from the pleat, then beg shaping neck: at neck edge on alt rows, transfer (10) 11 [12] sts, then (2) 3 [3] sts, then 1 st 3 times to a spare needle or stitch holder.

When piece measures (11½"/29cm) 13"/33cm [14½"/37cm] from beg, start shaping shoulder: BO on alt rows (5 sts 3 times) 5 sts twice, and 1 st 6 times [6 sts 3 times].

• Back

Work as for front to **.

Work even until piece measures (11½"/29cm) 13"/33cm [14½"/ 37cm], then start shaping shoulders and neck. For shoulders, BO at each side on alt rows, (5 sts 3 times) 5 sts twice and 6 sts once [6 sts 3 times], and for neck, put the (20) 24 [26] center sts on a spare needle or stitch holder and finish each side separately, transferring 4 sts to stitch holder at neck edge of 2nd row and 2 sts on 4th row.

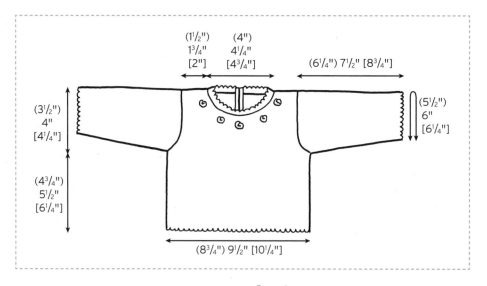

(1½") | (4")
1¾" | 4¼"
[2"] | [4¾"]

(6¼") 7½" [8¾"]

(3½")
4"
[4¼"]

(5½")
6"
[6¼"]

(4¾")
5½"
[6¼"]

(8¾") 9½" [10¼"]

• Sleeves

Using #3/3mm needles and A, CO (52) 54 [58] sts and work in Double Rib, inc 1 st (every 8 rows 6 times) every 6 rows, then 8 rows alternately 6 times [every 8 rows 9 times].

When piece measures (4¼"/11cm) 4¾"/12cm [5¼"/13cm], change to Stockinette St, still cont with the shaping.

When piece measures (5¼"/13cm) 6¼"/16cm [7½"/19cm], BO 4 sts at beg of next 2 rows, (2) 3 [3] sts at beg of next 2 rows, and 2 sts at beg of next 14 rows, then (3) 3 [4] sts at beg of next 2 rows. BO the rem (18) 22 [26] sts.

Finishing

Sew the shoulder and side seams of the dress.

Using A, pick up and K 18 sts along the side of the opening and work in Stockinette St: 1 row A, 2 rows B, 2 rows A, then BO. Rep on the other side, fold back the borders and sl st to WS.

Using A, transfer the (15) 17 [18] sts of left front neck to a #3/3mm dpn, then the (32) 36 [38] sts of the back neck and the (15) 17 [18] sts of the right front and work in Stockinette St: 1 row A, 2 rows B, and 2 rows A, then BO. Fold back the border and sl st to WS.

Sew seams of sleeves and set in armholes.

To make the bows, CO 68 sts in B and K 1 row, BO as you knit. Make 2 more cords in the same way. Make a little bow with each of these cords and sew one to each side of the top, 2"/5cm from the hem, and the 3rd at the point of the neck.

Sew snap fastener to edges of the front opening.

Sweater ★

Sizes

(3 months) 6 months [12 months]

Materials

Any 100% wool fingering weight yarn, such as Bouton d'Or's *Baby Superwash* (100% wool; 1¾oz/50g = 219yd/200m) in C (cream–*Naturel*/380)

3 months: 2 balls
6 months: 2 balls
12 months: 2 balls
14"/35cm of ⅜"/1cm pale gray satin ribbon
1 snap fastener
1 pair #3/3mm knitting needles, or size needed to obtain gauge
1 set #3/3mm double-pointed needles

Stitches

Stockinette Stitch: See pants instructions.
Picot edging: *Row 1:* K1, *yo, K2tog*, rep from * to *, K1. *Row 2:* P.

Gauge

See pants instructions.

Making the sweater

• Front

Using #3/3mm needles, CO (66) 72 [78] sts and work 2 rows in Stockinette St, then the 2 rows of Picot edging, and cont in Stockinette St until piece measures (5¼"/13cm) 6"/15cm [6¾"/17cm], then beg shaping armholes: BO 3 sts at beg of next 2 rows, then 2 sts at beg of next 2 rows and 1 st at beg of next 6 rows.**

   When piece measures (7"/18cm) 8¼"/21cm [9½"/24cm], beg shaping neck: BO the (8)12 [14] center sts of next row and finish each side separately, BO at neck edge of alt rows, 3 sts twice, 2 sts once, and 1 st 3 times.

   When piece measures (8¾"/22cm) 9¾"/25cm [11¼"/28cm], BO the rem (12) 13 [15] sts.

• Back

Work as for front to **.

   When piece measures (6¾"/17cm) 7¾"/20cm [9"/23cm], BO the 2 center sts of next row for the opening and finish each side separately.

   When piece measures (8½"/21.5cm) 9¾"/24.5cm [11"/27.5cm], beg shaping neck: BO 10 sts at neck edge, then (4) 6 [7] sts on next alt row.

   When piece measures (8¾"/22cm) 9¾"/25cm [11"/28cm], BO the rem (12) 13 [15] sts.

• Sleeves

Using #3/3mm needles, CO (42) 44 [48] sts and work 2 rows in Stockinette St, then the 2 rows of Picot edging, and cont in Stockinette St, inc 1 st at each end of (every 8 rows 6 times) every 6, then every 8 rows alternately 8 times [every 8 rows 9 times].

   When piece measures (6"/15cm) 7"/18cm [8¼"/21cm], BO 2 sts at beg of next 8 rows, then BO the rem (38) 44 [50] sts.

Finishing

Sew the shoulder and side seams of the sweater.

   Pick up and K (72) 80 [88] sts around the neck, and work 2 rows in Stockinette St, then work the 2 rows of Picot edging, then 3 rows in Stockinette St, then BO. Fold back this border and sl st to WS.

   Pick up and K 19 sts along one side of the back opening and work 6 rows in Stockinette St, then BO. Rep for the other side, then fold back these borders and sl st to WS.

   Sew snap fastener to the edges of the opening.

Sew seams of sleeves and set in armholes.
   Hem bottom of the sweater and around the cuffs.
   Cut the ribbon into 5 pieces and form the pieces into loose knots. Sew them around the edge of the front neck.

Tie-front sweater ★★

Sizes

(3 months) 6 months [12 months]

Materials

Any 100% wool fingering weight yarn, such as Bouton d'Or's *Baby Superwash* (100% wool; 1¾oz/50g = 219yd/200m) in colors: A (pale pink–Rosée/513) and C (cream–*Naturel/380*)
3 months: 2 balls C and a small amount of A
6 months: 2 balls C and a small amount of A
12 months: 3 balls C and a small amount of A
3 snap fasteners
1 pair #3/3mm knitting needles, or size needed to obtain gauge

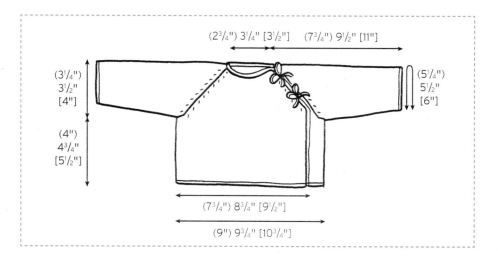

Stitches
Stockinette Stitch: See pants instructions.
Left-slanting decrease (SKP): Sl 1 knitwise, K1, PSSO.
Double decrease (SK2P): Sl 1 knitwise, K2tog, PSSO.

Gauge
See pants instructions.

Making the tie-front sweater

• Back
Using #3/3mm needles and C, CO (69) 75 [81] sts and work in
Stockinette St: 3 rows C, 2 rows A, 3 rows C, then make a hem on
the next row by knitting each st tog with the corresponding loop
from the CO row. Cont in C until piece measures (4¼"/11cm)
5½"/13cm [6"/15cm], then beg raglan shaping: BO 4 sts at beg
of next 2 rows, then at 1 st in from each end of alt rows, make
(*2 single dec, 1 dble dec*, rep from * to * 5 times in all)
* 2 single dec, 1 dble dec*, rep from * to * 5 times in all, then
2 single dec [*3 single dec, 1 dble dec*, rep from * to * 4 times
in all, then 3 single dec] (use K2tog or K3tog to dec on RH edge
and SKP or SK2P to dec on LH edge).

When piece measures (7"/18cm) 8¼"/21cm [9½"/24cm],
BO the rem (21) 23 [27] sts.

• Right front
Using #3/3mm needles and C, CO (60) 66 [72] sts, then work as
for back, making a hem and cont even in C until piece measures
(4¼"/11cm) 5¼"/13cm [6"/15cm]. Beg raglan shaping: at armhole
edge of 1st row BO 4 sts, then at 1 st in from edge on alt rows,
make (*2 single dec, 1 dble dec*, rep from * to * 4 times in all,
then make 1 single dec) *2 single dec, 1 dble dec*, rep from * to *
4 times in all, then make 3 single dec [*4 single dec, 1 dble dec*,
rep from * to * 3 times in all, then make 2 single dec].

When piece measures (5¼"/13cm) 6"/15cm [6¾"/17cm], beg

front raglan shaping: At 1 st in from RH edge of alt rows, make
(*1 single dec, 1 dble dec*, rep from * to * 5 times in all) *1 single
dec, 1 dble dec*, rep from * to * 5 times in all, then make 2 single
dec [*2 single dec, 1 dble dec *, rep from * to * 4 times in all,
then make 2 single dec] (use K2tog or K3tog to dec on RH edge
and SKP or SK2P to dec on LH edge).

When piece measures (6¼"/15.5cm) 7¼"/18.5cm
[8½"/21.5cm], BO the (10) 12 [16] center sts of next row for the
neck and finish each side separately, cont with the raglan
shaping. On alt rows, BO 2 sts at neck edge twice, then 1 st once,
then the 2 sts rem after the last dec for the raglan shaping.

• Left front
Work as for right front, reversing shapings.

• Right sleeve
Using #3/3mm needles and C, CO (40) 42 [46] sts, then work
as for back, making a hem and cont in C, inc 1 st at each edge
(every 4 rows 7 times) every 4 rows 9 times [every 4 rows
7 times, then every 6 rows 3 times].

When piece measures (4¾"/12cm) 6"/15cm [7"/18cm], beg
raglan shaping: BO 4 sts at beg of next 2 rows, then on the RH
edge make the same dec as for the LH edge of right front, and
on the LH edge, the same decs as for the back. After the last dec
for the front, BO at the RH edge of alt rows, (5 sts, then 4 sts)
6 sts, then 5 sts [8 sts, then 7 sts].

• Left sleeve
Work as for right sleeve, reversing shapings.

Finishing
Join raglan sleeve seams to front and back raglans and sew side
seams of jacket.

Using C, pick up and K (71) 83 [95] sts along the right front
edge and raglan edge, then work 6 rows in Stockinette St and BO.

Work a similar border on the left front.

Using C, pick up and K (73) 83 [93]sts around right neck, across top of sleeves, and around left neck, and work a similar border.

For each of the 2 bows, CO 68 sts in C and K 1 row, BO the sts as you knit.

Make a little bow from each of these cords and sew them to the raglan edge of the right front.

Sew a snap fastener on WS of the right front, underneath each of the bows, and on the matching halves on the left front.

Sew a snap fastener on the LH border at the left front neck and the matching half on WS of the right front.

Booties ★★

Sizes
3 months (6 months)

Materials
Any 100% wool fingering weight yarn, such as Bouton d'Or's *Baby Superwash* (100% wool; 1³/₄oz/50g = 219yd/200m) in colors: A (pale pink–*Rosée/513*), B (silver gray–*Glacier/231*), C (cream–*Naturel/380*), and D (taupe–*Taupe/570*)
For both sizes: ¹/₃oz/10g each in A, B, and C, and enough for a few rows of D
1 pair #3/3mm knitting needles, or size needed to obtain gauge
1 spare needle or stitch holder

Stitches
Stockinette Stitch: See pants instructions.
Garter Stitch: K every row.
Picot edging: See sweater instructions.
Left-slanting decrease (SKP): See jacket instructions.

Embroidery stitch
Bullion Knot: Bring needle up and draw yarn to RS of work, push needle back through work a short distance away, leaving a slack loop, then bring needle partway out again at original exit point. Twist thread of loop 6 or 7 times around needle, then pull it through, keeping coils tight between thumb and forefinger. Push needle back again through 2nd point and pull knot tight. Finish with a retaining st on WS.

Gauge
See pants instructions.

Making the booties
Begin with the sole. Using #3/3mm needles and B, CO 6 (8) sts and work in Garter St, inc 1 st at each end of alt rows 3 times.

When piece measures 2½"/6cm (2³/₄"/7cm), dec 1 st at each end of alt rows 3 times, then BO.

For the foot: CO 60 (66) sts in B and work 4 rows in Garter St, then change to A and work in Stockinette St until piece measures ³/₄"/2cm (1"/2.5cm), then beg the upper part of the bootie: K24 (26), K2tog, K8 (10), SKP, K24 (26). Cont dec in this way on alt rows 9 (10) times, keeping dec to either side of the 8 (10) sts that make the upper part of the bootie. At the same time, work 6 rows in Stockinette St, 4 rows in Garter St, then cont in Stockinette St, working the dec and the 8 (10) sts in the center in C and the side sts in A. Cont on rem 40 (44) sts.

On the next row, K15 (16), put the rem sts on a spare needle or stitch holder, and CO 10 sts to form the strap. K 2 rows in Garter St, then BO the 10 sts on the 3rd row. Put the rem 15 (16) sts on a spare needle or stitch holder.

Work a 2nd strap on the 1st 15 (16) sts of the other side. Return to the 10 (12) sts of the upper part of the bootie and work 2 rows in Stockinette St, dec 1 st at each end of 1st row, then replace all the sts on the needle and, using C, work next row as foll: K1, K2tog, K6 (7), K2tog, K3, K2tog, K6 (8), K2tog, K3, K2tog, K6 (7), K2tog, K1. Work 1¼"/3cm in Stockinette St on the rem 32 (36) sts, then work the 2 rows of Picot edging, then 2 rows in Stockinette St and BO.

Finishing
Sew the seam and attach the sole.

Fold back the top of the bootie to form the picot edge and sl st to WS.

Sew the ends of the 2 straps tog and embroider 2 Bullion Knots in B and 4 Bullion Knots in D.

Make a 2nd bootie in the same way.

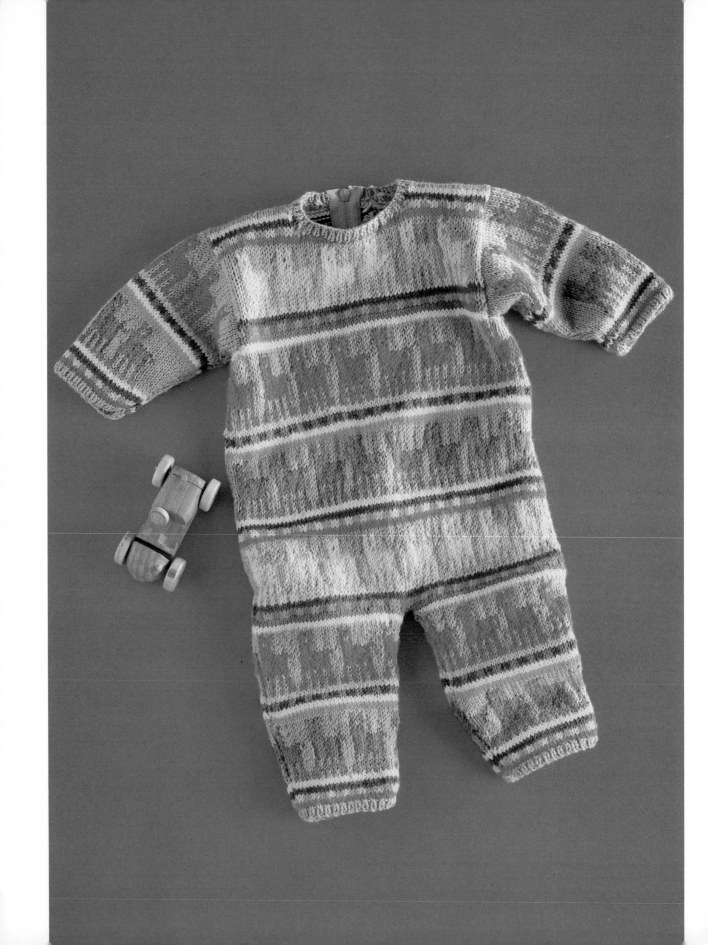

choosing and substituting yarns

The patterns in this book were each designed with a specific yarn in mind. If you substitute a recommended yarn, you should choose one with the same weight and a similar fiber content. You should always take the time to make a gauge swatch before you begin a pattern, but it's especially important to do so if you are substituting the suggested yarn. If necessary, change needle sizes to obtain the correct gauge.

Yarn weight categories	1 SUPER FINE	2 FINE	3 LIGHT	4 MEDIUM	5 BULKY	6 SUPER BULKY
Types of yarn in category	Sock, fingering, baby	Sport, baby	DK, light worsted	Worsted, afghan, aran	Chunky, craft, rug	Bulky, roving
Knit gauge range (St st to 4 inches)	27-32 sts	23-26 sts	21-24 sts	16-20 sts	12-15 sts	6-11 sts
Recommended needle sizes	#1-3/2.25-3.25mm	#3-5/3.25-3.75mm	#5-7/3.75-4.5mm	#7-9/4.5-5.5mm	#9-11/5.5-8mm	#11 and larger/ 8mm and larger

Adapted from the Standard Yarn Weight System of the Craft Yarn Council of America.

knitting abbreviations

alt	alternate
beg	beginning
BO	bind off
ch	chain stitch (yo, draw through loop on hook)
cm	centimeter(s)
cn	cable needle
CO	cast on
cont	continue
dble	double
dec	decrease/decreasing
dpn	double-pointed needle
foll	following
g	grams
Garter St	Garter Stitch
inc	increase/increasing
K	knit
K2tog	knit 2 sts together
K3tog	knit 3 sts together
LH	left-hand
M1	Make 1 (pick up and K or P loop between last st knitted and next st in LH needle
mm	millimeter(s)
Moss St	Moss Stitch
oz	ounces
P	purl
patt	pattern/patterns
PSSO	pass slip stitch over
P2tog	purl 2 sts together
rem	remainder/remaining
rep	repeat
RH	right-hand
RS	right side
sc	single crochet (inset hook in st, yo and draw yarn through loop, yo and draw yarn through both loops
SKP	left-slanting decrease (Sl 1 knitwise, K1, PSSO)
SK2P	double decrease (Sl 1 knitwise, K2tog, PSSO)
sl	slip
SL ST	slip stitch (insert hook in st, yo and draw yarn through both loops)
st, sts	stitch/es
Stockinette St	Stockinette Stitch
tog	together
WS	wrong side
wyib	with yarn in back
wyif	with yarn in front
yd	yards
yo	yarn over
yrn	yarn around needle
"	inch
*	repeat instructions after asterisk or between asterisks across row or as many times as instructed

list of projects

A detailed list of all the patterns … and the designers who created them.

smart babies

other needlearts books from Watson-Guptill

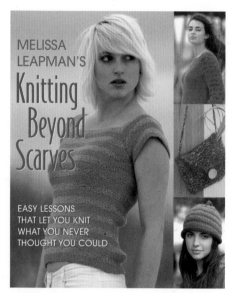

Melissa Leapman's
Knitting Beyond Scarves
Melissa Leapman

Knit with Beads: Stunning
Shawls & Wraps
Scarlet Taylor

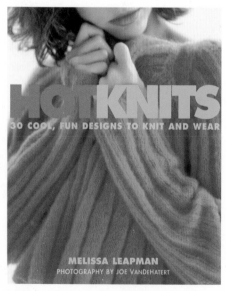

Hot Knits
Melissa Leapman

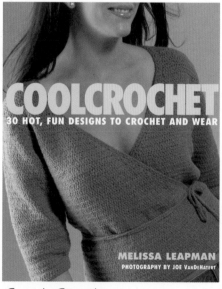

Cool Crochet
Melissa Leapman

crafts books
from Watson-Guptill

Beaded Macramé Jewelry
Sherri Haab

The Art of Feltmaking
Anne Vickrey

Designer Style Handbags
Sherri Haab

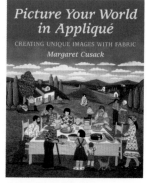

Picture Your World in Appliqué Margaret Cusack

Scrapbook Styles: Celebrate Your Stories Anita Louise Crane and Caroll Louise Shreeve

Collage with Color
Jane Davies

By the Batch: Creative Cards, Postcards, Envelopes & More Judi Kauffman

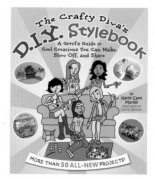

Paper for All Seasons
Sandra Lounsbury Foose

KnitGrrl
Shannon Okey

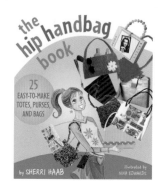

The Hip Handbag Book
Sherri Haab

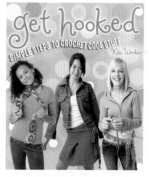

Get Hooked
Kim Werker

The Crafty Diva's D.I.Y. Stylebook Kathy Cano Murillo

about the author

Patricia Wagner is the editor-in-chief of *Modes & Travaux*, a leading French-language women's magazine that offers projects and practical information on fashion, crafts, cooking, health, and beauty. She lives in Paris.

about the photographer

Jean-François Chavanne is a commercial photographer based in Paris.

index